ELDERS IN EVERY CITY

The Origin and Role
of the Ordained Ministry

by Roger Beckwith

PATERNOSTER PRESS

First published 2003 by Paternoster Press

09 08 07 06 05 04 03   7 6 5 4 3 2 1

Paternoster Press is an imprint of Authentic Media,
PO Box 300, Carlisle, Cumbria CA3 0QS, UK
And Box 1047 Waynesboro, GA 30830-2047, USA
www.paternoster-publishing.com

British Library Cataloguing in Publication Data

A catalogue record for this book is available from the British Library

ISBN 1-84227-230-6

Cover design by 4-9-0 ltd.
Printed in Great Britain by
Cox and Wyman Ltd., Cardiff Road, Reading

To
James Innell Packer,
Presbyter
Mentor
and
Friend

CONTENTS

INTRODUCTION 5

1 THE PREFACE TO THE ANGLICAN ORDINAL 9

2 THE ORIGINAL PRESBYTER-BISHOP 11

3 MINISTRY: CHARISMATIC AND INSTITUTIONAL 15

4 THE THEORIES OF LIGHTFOOT AND KIRK 23

5 THE JEWISH PRESBYTER OR ELDER 28

6 FROM JEWISH PRESBYTER
   TO CHRISTIAN PRESBYTER-BISHOP 42

7 FROM PRESBYTER-BISHOPS
   TO BISHOP AND PRESBYTERS 55

8 THE DEACON 64

9 THE ORDAINED MINISTRY AND THE
   SACRAMENTS 69

10 SUBSEQUENT DEVELOPMENTS 75

11 LESSONS FOR TODAY 81

   BIBLIOGRAPHY 85

   INDEXES 93

INTRODUCTION

This small book began as a series of addresses given at Whalley Abbey to clergy of the Blackburn diocese in January 1984, at the invitation of the then Bishop of Lancaster, Dennis Page. The addresses, with all their imperfections, were so warmly received that I was encouraged to think of printing them, both for the original audience and for a wider public. Probably the original audience has, by this date, long given up any expectation of seeing them in print, but, now that they are at last appearing as a little book, I hope that its lengthy gestation will have made it a more healthy child.

The bishop allowed me to choose my own subject for the addresses, and the role of the ordained ministry was suggested by experience of teaching in theological colleges, first at Tyndale Hall, Bristol, and then at Wycliffe Hall, Oxford, and also by invitations that I had received to address clergy and ordinands elsewhere and to advise members of the General Synod about the matter. On the agenda of the General Synod the ordained ministry is a recurring theme, but there seemed to be as much uncertainty about it among the legislators as among those who practised this ministry or were preparing themselves to do so.

All this was well before the decision to ordain women as priests, which is not, therefore, a central theme of the book. At the time, I shared the common expectation that this question would remain purely theoretical in as traditional a church as the Church of England. Although that expectation has since been belied, it remains a much more basic question what is the role of the ordained ministry than who may rightly be admitted to it. If a clear answer is found for the first question, the second should answer itself.

The reasons why there has of late been so much uncertainty about the role of the ordained ministry are not far to seek. The widespread decline of Christian belief and practice in the western world has both reduced the number of clergy and ordinands, and increased soul-searching among those that there are. This is an international and interdenominational phenomenon. Secular society, even at its most reflective, is today anti-institutional and anti-hierarchical, and therefore tends to be anti-clerical. Clergy and ordinands cannot be oblivious of these attitudes or unaffected by them. Indeed, it is important for the effectiveness of their ministry that they should address these attitudes in an understanding way. The priest has progressively lost his position in society, both by becoming fewer in number and by finding some of his traditional roles in education, counselling, social welfare and marriage guidance taken over by teachers, doctors, psychiatrists, social workers and other experts who are without any necessary Christian convictions. Again, the clergy are no longer one of the recognised learned professions, and those who are learned among them tend to spend their whole working lives in universities and colleges and not any longer to engage much in parish ministry.

Within the church itself, the ordained ministry is also under challenge. It was once easy to think of the ordained ministry in terms of exclusive rights to perform certain functions, whether the celebration of holy communion and the pronouncement of absolution, as taught by the Council of Trent (session 23, chapter 1), or the whole ministry of the word and sacraments and the leading of public worship, as long practised in the Church of England. Today, the campaign for the ministry of the laity and the prevalence of the charismatic movement make the assumption of exclusive rights for the clergy much more problematic. Even the advent of universal education has made a difference, for the clergy's right to decide theological and religious issues is no longer undisputed. The question is now being asked, whether the clergy do not simply duplicate the role of the laity? Do they really have any distinctive role at all? And how did the belief arise that they do? Is it actually conceivable that such a belief could go back to the beginning and be grounded in Scripture? Is it not more likely that a gradual process of institutionalization, over the course of several generations, established the clergy in the position which they now hold, but which originally they did not?

Despite all this questioning, old attitudes still survive. The clericalism which has no true place for the laity, and sees the whole work of the church as being done by the clergy or not at all, still exists. It is not, of course, only a disease of the clergy: a supine laity has often viewed its clergy in just this way. But the attempt at omnicompetence by the clergy is inevitably a failure. Clericalism gives rise to the reaction of anti-clericalism, so this too is still with us. Anti-clericalism attempts to obliterate the distinction between clergy and laity, but tends to make an exception where personal interests are involved! If clericalism is particularly prevalent among Anglo-Catholics, anti-clericalism is particularly prevalent among evangelicals. And what is particularly prevalent among liberals is surely secularism. To say that *this* is still with us is an understatement. For the radical secularist, who has broken down all distinction between the church and the world, it goes without saying that he has broken down all distinction between the ordained and the unordained. The task of the clergy is for him no different from that of the laity, and the task of the

Christian no different from that of the pagan. It is very much a this-worldly task, primarily concerned with social welfare.

The author is under no illusion that he has been able to address all these attitudes and questionings, both within the church and without. His attempt is much more modest. He tries to show, for those (of any churchmanship) who are willing to be guided by the Scriptures, that the ordained ministry does find its origin there and not elsewhere, and that it is complementary to other ministries, not in competition with them. The author is aware that he is going over much old ground, and he does not pretend to be a great expert either in biblical or in patristic studies himself; he has simply attempted to learn from those who are. What is new in his book, he believes, is the serious attempt to bring the study of Judaism to bear upon this issue, so that the biblical and patristic evidence can be read against that significant contemporary background. If he has succeeded in this, he believes that it will throw a new light on the emergence and early development of the Christian ministry, which will answer many doubts and remove much uncertainty. If, in the process, it helps clergy and ordinands to see their own vocation with more clarity and conviction, this is what the writer has most of all hoped to achieve.

Incidentally, if the writer seems to be devoted to the *Book of Common Prayer* and its *Ordinal*, to the *Thirty-nine Articles* and the writings of Cranmer and Hooker, that is because he is. He sees them as the finest expressions of Anglicanism – of historic Christianity as reformed by the word of God.

CHAPTER ONE

THE PREFACE TO THE ANGLICAN ORDINAL

The preface to the *Ordinal* of the Church of England in the *Book of Common Prayer* states that 'It is evident unto all men diligently reading holy Scripture and ancient Authors, that from the Apostles' time there have been these Orders of Ministers in Christ's Church: Bishops, Priests, and Deacons.' This is a very carefully phrased statement which, through loose interpretation, has been misrepresented both by its defenders and by its critics.

For, in the first place, it does not say that this is evident to those 'diligently reading holy Scripture *or* ancient Authors' but to those 'diligently reading holy Scripture *and* ancient Authors'; in other words, it is evident from Scripture and the Fathers taken together, but not necessarily from one of the two taken singly. If we have difficulty finding the threefold ministry in the New Testament taken by itself, the preface does not say that we should be able to find it there.

In the second place, the preface does not say that '*by* the Apostles' *decision* there have been these Orders of Ministers in Christ's Church' but '*from* the Apostles' *time* there have been these Orders of Ministers in Christ's Church'; in other words, from the period before the last of the apostles died there have been three orders of ordained ministers; and the last of the apostles, St John, is stated by Irenaeus (*Against Heresies* 3:3:4) to have lived until the reign of Trajan, who did not become emperor till AD 98. Since the threefold ministry was widespread when Ignatius of Antioch was writing his letters, about AD 110, it can hardly have arisen later than the beginning of Trajan's reign, in other words, later than the end of the apostolic age. So the preface to the Ordinal is stating the simple truth in saying that it dates from the apostles' time. How far the apostles were *responsible* for the development which took place is left an open question.

In conformity with this, Hooker considered it simply a matter of probability that the first bishops were appointed by the apostles themselves (*Ecclesiastical Polity* 7:11:8), and, when discussing a passage of Jerome which seems to state the contrary, he has a marginal note expressing dissatisfaction with the attempt he has made in the text to explain it away (7:5:8). The test of what is certainly apostolic, for Hooker as for the historic Church generally, is whether it is found in the New Testament.

CHAPTER TWO

THE ORIGINAL PRESBYTER-BISHOP

Earlier in the apostolic age, as is well known, the presbyter-bishop seems to have been one and the same person. (The Greek word *presbuteros*, which is the etymological source of the English words 'presbyter' and 'priest', is in the English Bible normally translated 'elder' or 'old(er) man', but the frequent technical sense is brought out more clearly if one uses 'presbyter'.)[1] The identity of presbyter and bishop is hinted at in the traditional text of 1 Peter 5:2, where the presbyters are described as 'exercising the oversight' (literally, 'bishopping'), and it is made unmistakably clear in Acts 20:17,28, where Paul says to the 'presbyters' of Ephesus that the Holy Ghost made them 'bishops', and in Titus 1:5-7, where he says that he left Titus in Crete to appoint 'presbyters' in every city, if any man is blameless, for the 'bishop' must be blameless. 'Bishop' (Greek *episkopos*) means overseer, just as 'presbyter' means senior man, but in the New Testament this term too is beginning to have a technical sense, as is likewise the case with the third term 'deacon' (Greek *diakonos*), which basically

---

[1] The English Reformers, who denied that the Christian ministry is a sacrificing priesthood, retained the term 'priest' in the Prayer Book as a contraction of 'presbyter' (see Bishop Jewel, *Works*, Parker Society, vol. 4, p.911f.; Archbishop Whitgift, *Works*, Parker Society, vol. 3, p.350f; and others). This is etymologically correct, but involves an inevitable ambiguity, because the English Bible has no other word than 'priest' to translate the Hebrew and Greek terms for the sacrificing priest of Old Testament religion. 'Presbyter' avoids this ambiguity.

means servant.   Because of the original identity of the
presbyter and the bishop, we find the twofold expression
'bishops and deacons' in Philippians 1:1, and qualifications are
listed in 1 Timothy 3 for those to be appointed to the two
offices of 'bishop' and 'deacon', but not to any third office.[2]
The twofold expression 'bishops and deacons' is still found in
much of the earliest post-apostolic literature. It is used in
Didache (or Teaching of the Twelve Apostles) 15 and 1
Clement 42, about the end of the first century (see also 1
Clement 44, where 'presbyters' have 'episcopate'), while in the
Epistle of Polycarp 5, not very far into the second century, the
parallel twofold expression 'presbyters and deacons' is used.
In the Rome of Clement and the Smyrna of Polycarp, it is clear,
the writer of the epistle concerned already stands out from the
other bishops or presbyters of his city, but he still uses the
traditional language, which, as the letters of Ignatius show, was
rapidly changing elsewhere. Even Irenaeus, towards the end of
the second century, when the separate office of bishop was
well established, freely refers to bishops as 'the presbyters',
though he is equally ready to call them 'bishops' (*Against
Heresies* 4:26:2-5, referring back to the section 3:2:2 – 3:4:1).

The common origin of the two offices of bishop and
presbyter was not afterwards forgotten. Even the Council of
Trent, in session 23, appears to teach that the highest of the
seven orders of minister is the priest, which includes (as grades
within it) both bishop and presbyter. This accords with the fact
that the three major orders of the mediaeval church were not
deacon, priest and bishop, but subdeacon, deacon and

---

[2] It is surprisingly often asserted that in the Pastoral Epistles 'bishop'
occurs only in the singular and 'presbyters' only in the plural, but the total
number of occurrences of the two words is small, and 1 Tim. 5:19, where
'presbyter' is used in the singular, is an exception. Elsewhere in the New
Testament, 'bishops' occurs twice in the plural (Acts 20:28; Phil. 1:1).

presbyter-cum-bishop. And among the Reformers, our own Thomas Cranmer states that bishops and priests 'were not two things, but both one office in the beginning of Christ's religion'.[3] Because of his recognition of this fact, Cranmer used an epistle from Acts 20, with an alternative from 1 Timothy 3, when drawing up the Anglican service for the Ordering of Priests, despite the references these passages make to 'overseers' or 'bishops'. It was only in the revision of 1662, to stop the mouths of contentious Presbyterians (so it is believed), that a different epistle was substituted.

The separation of the presbyter-bishop into two offices was just one of many changes in the realm of church order which took place in the late apostolic or sub-apostolic church and which were rapidly followed throughout Christendom. These changes are not documented until they have already occurred, or at least are already under way, and the reasons which influenced those who made them are nowhere stated at the time, though they must have been sufficiently compelling to cause the change, once made, to be adopted universally. Probably the reasons were not in every case the same, though church discipline and the preservation of unity seem likely to have been the most common reasons. The other changes are the confinement of the celebration of the eucharist to bishops and their delegates, the separation of the eucharist from the agape (or love-feast), and the delay of baptism for a shorter or longer period after the candidate professes faith in Christ. All these seem to be departures from New Testament practice. Alongside the changes go certain new developments, likewise

---

[3] *Remains and Letters*, Parker Society, p.117. The elaborate Anglican report *Episcopal Ministry* (London: Church House Publishing, 1990, p.79) is quite mistaken in supposing the English Reformers ignorant of this fact. Hooker also is perfectly clear on the point (*Ecclesiastical Polity* 7:2:2; 7:5:1f: 7:9:1-4).

absent from the New Testament but made in the interests of edification, namely, the institution of additional holy days (besides the Lord's Day) and the adoption of the habit of describing the eucharist as the offering of a sacrifice (in whatever sense this was at first meant).

New Testament practice, in matters of church order, is of course 'written for our learning', like New Testament doctrine; but, unlike New Testament doctrine, it is not necessarily written for our direct imitation. In learning from it we need to discern the principles underlying it, and to ensure that we are still observing these, even if changing circumstances cause us to introduce changes of practice. The new or altered practices which were introduced by the late apostolic or sub-apostolic church, and which have largely commended themselves to Christians ever since, were doubtless duly controlled by New Testament principles, and can still be defended in terms of New Testament principles. Nevertheless, because not clearly apostolic, they are in extreme circumstances alterable, despite their antiquity; and though nearly all those listed above were maintained at the Anglican Reformation, the last of them (the habit of describing the eucharist as the offering of a sacrifice) was not, because of the way this language had been progressively re-interpreted and misapplied in the intervening centuries.[4]

---

[4] For a fuller discussion of these developments, see the author's study *The Principles of Christian Custom* (forthcoming), ch.2.

CHAPTER THREE

MINISTRY: CHARISMATIC AND INSTITUTIONAL

The statement of the Church of England, with which we began, that it intended to maintain the ordained ministry in the form which it had taken by the end of the apostolic period, leaves entirely open the question of what happened earlier in the apostolic period. As J.T. Burtchaell remarks, in his significant recent book, the consensus of (liberal) historians since the nineteenth century has been that, for the first two or three generations of Christian history, the Spirit was given free rein, so that the church remained without formal structures. Division and heresy were the threats which led to later institutionalization, and church life has never been so animated since.[5] On this understanding, even the presbyter-bishop has to be a later development, when charismatic enthusiasm began to subside, and the Acts of the Apostles and the Pastoral Epistles, which indicate the contrary, must be regarded as late and unhistorical.

This reconstruction has met with a sympathetic reception even from some conservative Christians, who are influenced either by the desire to revive the ministry of the laity or by the Charismatic Movement. However, reflection is apt to modify this sympathy. Exponents of the ministry of the laity, such as

---

[5] *From Synagogue to Church* (Cambridge: The University Press, 1992), p.xiii.

John Stott in his book *One People* (London: Falcon Books, 1969), tend to lay much stress on Ephesians 4, interpreting verse 12 in the way popularized by J. Armitage Robinson's commentary, as meaning that 'the work of ministering' is the task of 'the saints' (that is, Christians in general), for which they are equipped by four ministries of the word – apostles, prophets, evangelists and pastor-teachers.[6] This interpretation, which is followed in most of the recent translations, has a good deal to be said for it, but it has the effect not of excluding formal structures from church life, but of making them essential to it. For the twelve apostles and St Paul were clearly chosen and commissioned by Christ; the pastor-teachers are hard to distinguish from the ordained presbyter-bishops, who have precisely those two functions, of pastoral rule and teaching, assigned to them in the Pastoral Epistles; and the only one of these four ministries of the word which is definitely independent of outward commissioning is that of prophets. Similarly, the charismatic movement has been led by experience of the free exercise of charismatic gifts not to dispense with outward ordering but to emphasise it, so that church life may not degenerate into chaos. There are few Christian circles in which the ordained ministry is as authoritarian as it often is in the charismatic movement.

---

[6] If this interpretation is correct, the work of ministering by the saints seems to be taken up again in verses 15 and 16. Recent objectors to the interpretation are J.N. Collins (*Diakonia: Re-interpreting the Ancient Sources*, New York: OUP, 1990), who points out that in the New Testament *diakonia*, ministering, usually refers to the ministry of the word, and Donald Robinson ('Ministry/Service in the Bible', in *Forward in Faith?* ed. David Robarts, Enmore: Aquila Books, 1998), who points out that *katartismos*, equipping, does not elsewhere in ancient Greek literature govern the preposition *eis*. The latter point seems the stronger, though it should be noted that the cognate verb, *katartidzo*, does govern the preposition *eis* in Rom. 9:22 and elsewhere.

It is therefore reasonable to ask whether the basic assumption underlying the liberal reconstruction of primitive Christianity, namely, that the free exercise of spiritual gifts and formal structures cannot co-exist but are mutually exclusive, is not a simplistic mistake? May it not rather be the case that the exercise of varieties of gifts by Christians in general, what is often called 'every-member ministry', *demands* formal structures, if it is to be fruitful? The two certainly co-exist in the New Testament books which the reconstructionists assume to be late and unhistorical. What book has more to say about charismatic phenomena than the Acts of the Apostles? And they are not absent from the Pastoral Epistles either (see 1 Tim. 1:18; 4:1,14). Even in the admittedly early Pauline letters, no case for an absence of formal structures can be established. For Paul's own apostolic authority is everywhere present, and even when other offices are not mentioned, they seem to be implied. Two of the spiritual gifts listed in Romans 12 and 1 Corinthians 12 are 'rule' and 'governments', which would need officers to exercise them. In the very free charismatic service of 1 Corinthians 14, Paul repeatedly calls for an introduction of 'order' and 'edification'. And the address to the church at the beginning of Philippians explicitly names 'the bishops and deacons', the same officers as we find in the Pastoral Epistles.[7] The New Testament picture is broadly uniform. So to divide up the New Testament according to its different authors, in the

---

[7] Harnack objects that the Greek article is not used before 'bishops' and 'deacons' in Phil. 1:1 (*The Constitution and Law of the Church in the First Two Centuries*, ET, London: Williams & Norgate, 1910, p.57), but the combination of the two titles must be significant, which would mean that the article is intended to be understood.

now fashionable manner, and to treat them as reflecting
independent practices,[8] is merely misleading.

The continuance of a full range of charismatic gifts at the
end of the first century and in the first half of the second
century is chiefly attested by the Didache and by the *Shepherd*
of Hermas, itself professedly a revelatory or prophetic book.
There are also the historical references to Ammia and
Quadratus as prophets in an anonymous writer cited by
Eusebius (*Ecclesiastical History* 5:17:2-4), but no further
details are given. The Didache and Hermas, like the New
Testament writers, know institutional ministries as well.
Didache 15 speaks of the appointment of 'bishops and
deacons' and ranks them with the charismatic 'prophets and
teachers' (cp. Acts 13:1) as fulfilling similar roles. Didache 11
speaks also of 'apostles', though apparently only meaning
itinerant prophets. It is noteworthy that false prophets are at
least as prominent in the experience of the author of the
Didache as are true (11f), and when we come to Justin Martyr
in the mid-second century, they seem to be *more* prominent
(*Dialogue with Trypho* 82). Hermas groups together 'apostles
and bishops and teachers and deacons', or 'prophets and
deacons', 'apostles and teachers', as building-stones of the
church (Vision 3:5; Similitude 9:15f), but notes that some have
already fallen asleep. Elsewhere he speaks of 'the presbyters
that preside over the church' (Vision 2:4). It seems that change
was under way. A Christian section of the Ascension of Isaiah,
thought to have been written at the end of the first century,
confirms this. It laments the sins of 'presbyters and pastors',
'pastors and presbyters', and the fact that now there are 'not

---

    [8] As is done, for example, by Eduard Schweizer (*Church Order in the New
Testament*, ET, London: SCM, 1961). Another detailed survey, but with much
less insistence on diversity, is Jean Delorme (ed.), *Le Ministère et les
Ministères selon le Nouveau Testament* (Paris: Editions du Seuil, 1974).

many prophets, nor those who speak reliable words, except one here and there in different places' (Ascension of Isaiah 3:21-31).

It is no way surprising that these writers laid special emphasis on the gift of prophecy, now becoming more rare. Apart from apostleship, it had been the spiritual gift most valued by Paul (1 Cor. 12:28; 14:1; 1 Thes. 5:19f), who says that it provided edification, encouragement and consolation (1 Cor. 14:3). Nevertheless, its disappearance in the second century was steady. As has rightly been said, Irenaeus, towards the end of the century, 'is the last writer who can still think of himself as belonging to the eschatological age of miracle and revelation';[9] and the Montanists, who tried to prolong the era of prophecy, only succeeded in convincing the church that this gift, like that of apostleship, belonged to the past. Healing is still found in the third century, but not prophecy.

1 Corinthians 12:11 emphasises that the Holy Spirit is not committed to act uniformly but distributes his gifts to each one severally 'even as he will'; and Ephesians 2:20 (cp. 3:5) makes the apostles and New Testament prophets part of the 'foundation' of the church, probably indicating that their role was not only basic but was also exercised once for all. If so, such revelatory gifts were given for a time only, under the New Testament dispensation no less than under the Old, and their permanent operation is through written records. How far this applies to other charismatic gifts, some of which attested the ministry of the apostles (Rom. 15:18f; 2 Cor. 12:11f; Heb. 2:4), is a matter for discussion; but it would not apply to them all. Teaching, which ranks third among the gifts (1 Cor. 12:28), is a

---

[9] Henry Chadwick, *The Early Church* (revised edn., London: Penguin, 1993), p.53. Cp. Irenaeus, *Against Heresies* 2:31:2; 2:32:4; 5:6:1.

ministry of permanent importance, exercised by presbyter-
bishops but not therefore confined to them; and the same
permanent importance belongs, in the nature of the case, to
exhorting, giving, ruling and showing mercy, in the list of
Romans 12 (verses 7, 8), and to the word of wisdom, the word
of knowledge, faith, helps and governments, in the lists of 1
Corinthians 12 (verses 8, 9, 28). They may be humbler gifts
than apostleship and prophecy, but Paul reminds us that they
are just as necessary (1 Cor. 12:12-27).

Alongside the charismatic ministries stand the institutional
ministries, and according to the New Testament account the
two stand alongside each other from the earliest stage.
Unequalled in importance among the institutional ministries
are the apostles of the Lord, the Twelve and St Paul, chosen
and commissioned by Jesus himself.[10] Of hardly less antiquity,
according to the Acts of the Apostles, are the elders or
presbyters, otherwise called bishops, who are found in the
Jerusalem church at least as early as Acts 11:30, and are
appointed by Paul and Barnabas, on their first missionary
journey, in all their newly formed missionary congregations
(Acts 14:23). The significance of this ministry is underlined in
four ways.

(i)   In many parts of the New Testament presbyter-bishops,
      sometimes assisted by deacons, are singled out from
      other ministries as having a unique position. In Acts
      14:23 and Titus 1:5 elders are the only church officers
      said to be appointed; in 1 Timothy 3:2-13 and Titus 1:6-
      9 there are lists of qualifications for these ministries
      alone, doubtless with a view to appointment; in Acts 15

---

[10] The name 'apostle' is occasionally extended to some others – James,
who had also 'seen Jesus our Lord' (1 Cor. 15:7; Gal. 1:19; cp. 1 Cor. 9:1),
Barnabas (Acts 14:4,14), who is perhaps thought of as an apostle of the church
of Antioch (Acts 13:2f; cp. 2 Cor. 8:23), and possibly to one or two more.

and elsewhere the elders hold a special place next to the apostles at the Jerusalem 'council' and in the life of the Jerusalem church; in Acts 20 elders alone are summoned from Ephesus to receive Paul's last instructions to the church; in Philippians 1:1 bishops and deacons alone are singled out in Paul's greeting to the church; in James 5:14 elders alone are to be summoned to the sick man's bedside to pray for him; in 1 Peter 5:1-4 the elders are separately addressed, as a group with unique responsibilities. Not just in the churches evangelised by Paul, but at Jerusalem itself, and in the churches with which James and Peter are in touch, presbyter-bishops hold this specially important role.

(ii) The name 'elder' or 'presbyter', unlike all other terminology used of the various ministries in the church, is not descriptive of function but simply indicates seniority. The application of this honorific term to those who exercise a particular ministry within the congregation, and to no-one else except those who are literally senior in age or in the faith, cannot be without significance.

(iii) Then again, elders and deacons are among the few ministries which require outward appointment by the church as well as a gift from God (Acts 14:23; Tit. 1:5; and the lists of qualifications necessary for appointment in 1 Tim. 3 and Tit. 1). These ministries likewise demand spiritual gifts (especially of teaching and pastoral oversight), but they involve ecclesiastical appointment as well. So they are not just ministries but also offices. Others may possess and exercise these particular gifts, but elders and deacons are publicly commissioned to exercise them; which helps to ensure that such important functions are indeed performed, and to give those who perform them some protection against unruly opponents.

(iv) Finally, the title 'elder', and the substance of the office, is by common consent taken over from Judaism. The synagogue elders of Luke 7:3, elsewhere in the Gospels called 'scribes' (Scripture scholars), 'teachers of the Law' or 'lawyers', but in the rabbinical literature regularly called 'elders' (Heb. *zaken*) or 'wise men', 'sages' (Heb. *hakam*), were the popularly recognised teachers in the Jewish community, men learned in the Scriptures, and often ordained by their own teachers with the laying-on of hands. Being taken over from Judaism, the eldership is probably one of the oldest elements in Christianity, not one of the youngest, and there is no reason why the Acts of the Apostles should be judged unhistorical for putting it so early. Among much that was new in Christian ministry, the eldership was old, but because it provided for needs that were as real in Christianity as in Judaism, particularly the need of regular instruction in revealed truth and godly living, it was retained with a minimum of adaptation in its new setting.[11]

---

[11] Those few writers who deny the connection with Judaism have to devise speculative explanations for the similarity of function and the identity of name, though they do not always recognise how close these links are. An example is R.A. Campbell, *The Elders: Seniority within earliest Christianity* (Edinburgh: T. & T. Clark, 1994), where no account is taken of the crucial rabbinical evidence. So also with his article 'The Elders of the Jerusalem Church', in *The Journal of Theological Studies*, NS, vol. 44:2 (Oct. 1993), pp.513-28.

CHAPTER FOUR

THE THEORIES OF LIGHTFOOT AND KIRK

To return to the matter of the separation of the presbyter-bishop into two offices, there are competing theories about the way that this took place. Bishop Lightfoot's theory is that the separate bishop originated by elevation from the presbyterate, while the theory of Bishop Kirk and his collaborators is that the separate presbyter originated by delegation from the essential ministry of the apostolate and episcopate.[12] The reasons for the separation, according to Lightfoot, were various. For one thing, a college of presbyters naturally needs a president; secondly, there was the example of James the Lord's brother as the single head of the mother church of Jerusalem; and thirdly, Jerome several times states that the reason one presbyter was placed over the rest, as bishop, was to counter tendencies to schism. Where this first took place, Lightfoot argues, was probably the Roman province of Asia, in western Turkey, since the evidence for bishops there is unusually abundant and early; and in Asia it may be attributed to the influence of St John, though elsewhere it would be due to imitation of the Asian practice. Most of Lightfoot's case is strong, and his conjecture

---

[12] See J.B. Lightfoot, *The Christian Ministry* (London: Macmillan, 1901), p.24f; K.E. Kirk, ed., *The Apostolic Ministry* (London: Hodder & Stoughton, 1946), p.8f. Lightfoot's treatise first appeared in his commentary on Philippians, published in 1868. Another older work which, for its historical information, is still of value, is H.B. Swete, ed., *Essays on the Early History of the Church and the Ministry* (London: Macmillan, 1918).

about Asia and St John is distinctly possible; though one
should remember that John's action would have been an
example, rather than a command, still less a command recorded
in the New Testament.[13]

Bishop Kirk and his team do not so much explain why the
separate presbyter emerged from the presbyter-bishop, as deny
that the offices were ever united. The burden of proving this is
committed to Austin Farrer, who makes a valiant effort, though
admitting that appearances are against him;[14] but, on the
assumption that he has made out his case, Bishop Kirk sums up
their reconstruction of what happened as follows. The ministry
of the word and sacraments, and the power of ordination, at
first rested with the apostles; the apostles ordained the earliest
presbyters, as a dependent ministry; they then ordained
bishops, as a supervisory ministry, like their own; and with
these bishops and their successors rested, from then on, the
chief responsibility for the word and sacraments and all future
ordinations.

This account,[15] though slightly complex, is not in itself
implausible: the difficulty arises when one asks on what

---

[13] Lightfoot, *op cit.*, pp.25-7, 39-42, 48-52. Other fourth-century writers,
besides Jerome, who continue to recognise that bishop and presbyter were
originally one, include Ambrosiaster, Chrysostom and Theodore of
Mopsuestia. Their statements are assembled by T.G. Jalland in his contribution
to *The Apostolic Ministry*, pp.320-34.

[14] *The Apostolic Ministry*, pp.150-70. An earlier writer who denied the
original identity of presbyter and bishop was Edwin Hatch (*The Organization
of the Early Christian Churches*, Bampton Lectures, 3rd ed., London:
Rivingtons, 1888). Hatch looked more to pagan precedents than Jewish, and
his ideas were further developed by Harnack. However, the implausibility of
denying what is so clear undermines all such theories. In Harnack's book *The
Constitution and Law of the Church in the First Two Centuries*, p.58, he
suggests that the two titles may be independently derived from the 'municipal
constitutions'; however, even he prefers the more moderate view that
'presbyter' is derived from Judaism and 'bishop' arose spontaneously.

[15] *The Apostolic Ministry*, pp.7-14.

evidence it rests, and whether the available evidence does not in some points conflict with it. We have already seen that bishop and presbyter seem originally to have been one office, not two. Also, New Testament evidence for the administration of the sacraments by the apostles is almost entirely lacking. Peter commands converts to be baptized, rather than personally baptizing them (Acts 10:48); Paul points out how few of his converts he has himself baptized (1 Cor. 1:13-17); and the commission to administer the other sacrament, 'do this in remembrance of me', is addressed to the same people as partake of it (1 Cor. 11:25), the people who at once bless the cup, break the bread and partake (1 Cor. 10:16f.). Though the Lord commissioned his apostles to celebrate the sacraments (Matt. 28:19; Lk. 22:19; 1 Cor. 11:24f.), they evidently felt free to follow his own example (Jn. 4:1f.) and to delegate the task. When we enquire for evidence that the apostles ordained the first bishops, we are pointed by Bishop Kirk and his colleagues to the Pastoral Epistles and 1 Clement, writings which in fact speak of a twofold ministry and not a threefold. And even if, as is clearly the case, Timothy and Titus themselves, or Clement himself, exercise a supervisory ministry, they do not do it as 'bishops', in any sense which distinguishes bishops from presbyters. Indeed, Timothy's stay in Ephesus (1 Tim. 1:3; 2 Tim. 1:18) may have been no longer than Paul's, since he subsequently seems to have left (2 Tim. 4:12); and the same may apply to Titus's stay in Crete (Tit. 1:5).

Diotrephes (3 Jn. 9-11), who has sometimes been thought of as a bishop, may simply have been an upstart presbyter-bishop, an arrogant colleague of Demetrius (verse 12). He certainly does not seem to have been appointed bishop by St. John.

The apostles, says Clement, writing about AD95, 'appointed their first fruits, when they had proved them by the Spirit, to be bishops and deacons unto them that should believe' (1 Clement

42). But this tells us precisely nothing as to when and how the 'bishops' they appointed were subsequently subdivided into bishops and presbyters. We only know that the latter development was well under way by the time Ignatius wrote his epistles, early in the second century, and that by the same time the eucharist also was being brought under the bishop's supervision: as Ignatius urges, 'Let that be reckoned a valid (*bebaia*) eucharist which is under the bishop or one to whom he shall have committed it' (*Smyrnaeans 8*). We are not told that at this stage the bishop would commit it only to presbyters, as was ultimately to be the case, and for a time there were certain alternative possibilities.[16] By about the mid-fourth century, however, alternatives were at an end, and the rule that only bishops and presbyters celebrated communion had become absolute, though baptism and the ministry of the word remained outside the same strict control. It all seems a more gradual process than Bishop Kirk envisages.

There have, of course, been other studies of the origin of episcopacy since Lightfoot and Kirk, but they all build upon the same scanty New Testament and patristic evidence, and

---

[16] The alternatives were prophets (Didache 10), confessors (Hippolytus, *Apostolic Tradition* 9) and laymen (Tertullian, *Exhortation to Chastity* 7), but the last only when no clergy were available. Already in this passage of Tertullian, however, presbyters are called 'priests' (*sacerdos*), just as bishops are elsewhere called by Tertullian 'high priests' (*summus sacerdos*, *On Baptism* 17); and much the same usage is found soon afterwards in Hippolytus (*Apostolic Tradition* 3, 8). There can be little doubt that this language is a consequence of the description of the eucharist as the offering of a sacrifice (which begins with 1 Clement 44 and Didache 14 about a hundred years earlier), and implies that bishops and presbyters are now the normal celebrants of the eucharist. T.G. Jalland (in *The Apostolic Ministry*, ed. K.E. Kirk, ch.5), tries to differentiate between the bishop and the presbyter in this matter, claiming that presbyters are not called 'priests' until the late fourth century; but all that may legitimately be claimed is that they did not so frequently need to exercise their 'priesthood' before that period, by celebrating communion, since they were still grouped round the city-bishop.

therefore reach equally disputable conclusions. It does not seem to the present writer that any improvement in the situation can be expected until the available evidence is increased, by taking account of the Jewish evidence as well. This is in fact more ample than is usually supposed. Both Lightfoot and Kirk, and most other writers also, recognize that Christian presbyters or elders were modelled on the elders of the synagogue. But, having recognized this fact, they fail to build upon it to any effect, and what they do say cannot be relied upon. We will now attempt to make a start in remedying this defect.

CHAPTER FIVE

THE JEWISH PRESBYTER OR ELDER

The term 'elder', both in Hebrew and Greek, has the basic sense of 'old(er) man', in which sense the Hebrew *zaken* is used in Genesis 25:8; 1 Kings 12:8; Psalm 148:12; Proverbs 17:6; Jeremiah 31:13, etc., and the Greek *presbuteros* in Acts 2:17; 1 Timothy 5:1. This suggests that originally elders were men of advancing years; and that the same still tended to be the case in New Testament times is shown by the Mishnah, which says that 'at sixty, one is fit to be an elder' (Aboth 5:21), and by 1 Peter 5:1-5, which says, 'the elders therefore among you I exhort ... Tend the flock of God, exercising the oversight ... Likewise, ye younger, be subject unto the elder'.

Throughout the Bible, seniority entitles people to respect (Lev. 19:32; 1 Tim. 5:1; 1 Pet. 5:5) and age is thought of as bringing experience and therefore wisdom (1 Kings 12:6-15; Prov. 4:1; 5:1). Consequently, the leading men of Israel, right through its Old Testament history, are the elders of the nation (Ex. 3:16,18; Lev. 4:15; Jdg. 21:16; 1 Sam. 4:3; 2 Sam. 3:17; 1 Kings 8:1,3; 2 Kings 23:1; 1 Chron. 11:3; Ezr. 5:5, 9; Jer. 26:17; Ezk. 8:1, etc.). Along with the priests, they are entrusted with the written Law, and charged to read it to the people (Deut. 31:9-13). When the people settle in the promised land, and are dispersed throughout its cities, the elders of the cities act as judges there (Deut. 19:12; 21:19f; 22:15-18; Josh. 20:4; Ruth 4:2,4,9,11; 1 Kings 21:8,11; 2 Kings 10:1, 5), thus continuing the practice of having lay judges for lesser questions, which began in the wilderness (Ex. 18:13-26; Deut. 1:9-18). The appeal judges at Jerusalem, however, are partly lay, partly priestly (Deut. 17:8-13; 2 Chron. 19:8-11).[17]

The lay judges of Exodus 18 and Deuteronomy 1 are selected for their wisdom, piety and integrity. Similarly, the choice made among the elders in Numbers 11:16-30, so that seventy of them may share the burden of ruling with Moses, probably reflects a recognition that age does not bring wisdom invariably. Indeed, a wise youth is better than a foolish old king (Eccles. 4:13). And one who studies and obeys God's Law has more understanding than the aged (Ps. 119:100). This recognition continues in the intertestamental literature. Wisdom befits the aged, and elders ought to be wise (Ecclus. 6:34; 8:8f; 25:3f,), but even the young are honoured if wise (Wisdom 4:8f., 13; 8:10) and are treated as elders (Susanna 45, 50). Judges are men specially selected from among the elders (Susanna 5f., 41), and so too are rulers. In 1 Maccabees 12:35, the elders of the people who consult together with Jonathan Maccabaeus are clearly a chosen ruling council of the nation. This council comes to be called the *gerousia*, eldership (Judith 4:8; 1 Macc. 12:6; 2 Macc. 1:10; Acts 5:21; also Antiochus III in Josephus, *Antiquities* 12:3:3, or 12:138). In Judith 6:14-16; 8:10f; 10:6, the three named rulers of the city are themselves elders, but on occasion they call together the whole body of the elders. In the view of Josephus, a city should have seven rulers or judges, assisted by two officers from the tribe of Levi (*Antiquities* 4:7:14,38, or 4:214,287; *War* 2:20:5, or 2:570f), the latter perhaps to provide that expert knowledge of

---

[17] For the Old Testament period, the Old Testament itself is our only authority. This is borne out by Hanoch Reviv's rather opaque sociological account, *The Elders in Ancient Israel: a Study of a Biblical Institution* (Jerusalem: Magnes Press, 1989). Neighbouring nations also had elders, as the Old Testament itself witnesses (Gen. 50:7; Num. 22:4, 7).

the Law of Moses which the Old Testament expects the priests
and Levites to possess.

The choosing of rulers and judges from among the elders,
according to their wisdom and probity, and the treating of even
the young as elders if they possessed the same qualities, led in
the intertestamental period to a situation where eldership was a
seniority acquired as much in other ways as it was by years.
Thus, the elders said to have been chosen from each tribe to
translate the Pentateuch into Greek are marked not so much by
age (Letter of Aristeas 122, 318) as by virtuous life and by
knowledge and understanding of the Law of Moses (32, 121f.,
321). They include both laymen and priests (184, 310), but
now with a large lay majority – a fact which calls for a word of
explanation.

After the return from the Exile, the work of Ezra the Scribe
had placed the Pentateuch at the centre of national life, with
much less of the previous distractions of syncretism. The study
of the Pentateuch became the primary qualification of the new
succession of 'scribes' (or Scripture-scholars) which Ezra
inaugurated. Ezra was himself a priest, which was appropriate,
because the priests and Levites had a special duty to teach the
Law of Moses (Lev. 10:10f; Deut. 33:10; Mal. 2:6f. etc.), as
well as to judge cases by it. However, for reasons of which we
cannot be sure, but probably because the priests and Levites
chose to concentrate on their ceremonial duties, in the
following centuries the study and teaching of Scripture was
taken over almost entirely by laymen, who came to be known
as elders. In the early second century BC, Ben Sira speaks of
wise 'scribes' (Ecclus. 38:24 - 39:11), wise 'elders' (Ecclus.
6:34; 8:8f.; 25:3-6) and 'wise men' (Ecclus. 3:29; 18:27-9;
27:11f.; 37:22-6) without any apparent distinction. In the
Alexandria of the first century AD we still find priests as well
as elders teaching on occasion, by expounding the Scriptures to

the people in the synagogue on the sabbath (Philo, *Hypothetica* 7:13), but in Palestine the task of teaching seems to have passed over entirely to the elders, who are called by this name in Luke 7:3, in a Jerusalem synagogue inscription of the period (the famous Theodotus inscription), and regularly in the rabbinical literature,[18] but in the New Testament are usually called 'scribes', 'teachers of the Law' or 'lawyers'.[19] They are addressed by the title 'rabbi'. The fact that the people were used to being taught by the scribes or elders is reflected in Matthew 7:29, where we are told that Jesus taught the people as one having authority, and 'not as their scribes'. Though their work is voluntary, they have achieved a recognised position in society almost equal to that of the priesthood. The elders teach on occasion in the Temple (Lk. 2:46) but have their great centre of influence in the local synagogues (Matt. 23:6; Mk. 1:21f; Lk. 5:17; 6:6f; 7:3-5; Jn. 12:42), where they could reach people much more readily. By the first century, as literary and archaeological evidence shows, there were

---

[18] See the article 'Elder: in the Talmud' in the *Encyclopaedia Judaica*, by L.I. Rabinovitz. Examples of this use of the term 'elder' in the Mishnah are Maaser Sheni 5:9; Shabbath 16:8; Sanhedrin 11:1f. The other common title for elders in the rabbinical literature is 'wise men, sages'. The elders of a synagogue would not necessarily have been confined to the teaching elders who belonged there, but no doubt included them. See L.I. Levine, *The Ancient Synagogue* (New Haven: Yale University Press, 2000), p.407f.

[19] The title which the New Testament does not use for Jewish teachers, understandably, is 'wise men, sages': this is reserved for Christian teachers (Matt. 23:34). The term 'scribe' is found in the rabbinical literature also, used either for a scholar and teacher of the past (though not of the present, as in the New Testament) or for a writer of biblical scrolls. The phrases 'the words of the scribes' and 'enjoined by the scribes' (meaning the teachers following Ezra, though now belonging to the past) occur repeatedly in the Mishnah, but contemporary teachers are usually called 'elders' or 'sages, wise men'. For a wide-ranging collection of evidence on the use of the term 'scribe' in the post-exilic period, see Christine Schams, *Jewish Scribes in the Second-Temple Period* (Sheffield: JSOT Supplement Series 291, 1998).

synagogues virtually everywhere in the Roman world where any substantial number of Jews were living, and services were held there every sabbath day (cp. Acts 13:14-44; 15:21). The fact that few synagogues dating from the first century have been excavated perhaps means that (like the oldest Christian churches) they tended at first to be built of less durable materials than stone. Nevertheless, putting archaeological and literary evidence together, in almost a score of places in Judaea synagogues dating from the first century have been identified, and in the Dispersion many more, dating from even earlier times.[20]

It used to be thought that the synagogue was wholly controlled by the Pharisaic scribes, but it is now realised that it originally had much independence. The synagogue belonged to the townsfolk themselves (Mishnah, Nedarim 5:5; Tosephta, Baba Metzia 11:23), and before the destruction of the Temple in AD 70 the Pharisees were simply the most influential school of religious thought among the Jews, not the only one,[21] and the other schools of thought also had their scribes or elders (Acts 4:5; 23:6-9). Synagogue practices, decorations and targums could diverge widely from rabbinical norms, and when, after AD 70, the beth ha-midrash, in which the rabbis expounded, became a separate place from the synagogue, a certain coolness could grow up between them.[22] It would be a mistake, however, to draw extreme conclusions from these

---

[20] See L.I. Levine, *The Ancient Synagogue*, chs. 3, 4. This book is a most valuable compendium of information.

[21] That the Pharisees, contrary to what is sometimes supposed, were the largest and most influential school of religions thought among the Jews, and also the earliest in their origins, see the chapter 'Judaism between the Testaments: the Stages of its Religious Development' in my book *Calendar and Chronology, Jewish and Christian* (Leiden: Brill, 1996), esp. pp. 170-2, 182-6.

[22] See L.I. Levine, *The Ancient Synagogue*, ch. 13.

facts. The Pharisaic elders needed the synagogue, and the synagogue needed the Pharisaic elders, and the relationship between them was bound, on the whole, to be close.

As a result of these developments, 'elder' becomes a word with various nuances, between which it easily moves. Basically, (i) it still means an old(er) man; but it can also (ii) mean a man selected from the other elders (or even from outside their number) as a ruler or judge, because of his character and abilities; and thirdly (iii) it can mean a man specially qualified to be a judge, and also a teacher, because of his special study of the Mosaic Law. Each possesses seniority, and therefore honour, but for differing reasons. Nor do these exhaust the meanings of the word. Other extensions of the first meaning are (iv) an older believer, especially one who could remember the great events of the Exodus (Josh. 24:31; Jdg. 2:7; Mishnah, Aboth 1:1) and (v) a man of old time (Heb. 11:2; cp. Matt. 15:2, 'the tradition of the elders', though here there is also a hint of the third meaning; and perhaps Rev. 4:4 etc.).

At Jerusalem, the ancient link between the elders and priests continued (Lam. 1:19; 4:16; 1 Macc. 7:33; 11:23) and it is prominent in the New Testament (Matt. 21:23; 26:3, 47; 27:1, 3, 12, 20; 28:11f; Acts 4:23; 23:14; 25:15). Out of the link has now grown the Sanhedrin, which is the ruling council of the nation and its supreme court of justice, presided over by the high priest. Elders and chief priests are included among its seventy-one members (Matt. 27:1; Mk. 8:31; 14:53; 15:1; Lk. 22:66; Acts 4:5, 8, 23; 22:5), along with 'scribes' and 'rulers', and these are terms which, as we have seen, probably have very similar meanings to the other two.

In rabbinical literature, the primary duty of the third class of elder (the teaching elder) is still to be a judge, and this is doubtless why we read in the New Testament of excommunications from the synagogue (Jn. 9:22; 12:42; 16:2), and of punishments being inflicted in the synagogue (Matt. 23:34; Mk. 13:9; Acts 22:19; 26:11). The normal number of judges for a case, according to the Mishnah, was three, with greater numbers for more serious offences or more eminent offenders (Sanhedrin 1), and these judges were doubtless selected from among the local community rulers and teaching elders. A *baraita*, or ancient quotation, of Mishnaic date, in the Talmud states that, while the Temple still stood, documents were sent from the Sanhedrin appointing men of wisdom and humility, who were esteemed by their fellow men, as local judges (Bab. Sanhedrin 88b). This looks like the confirmation of a local choice. The *baraita* also states that, from the local courts, judges were promoted to the higher courts[23].

In addition to the rulers of the local community, the *archons*, the synagogue had its own synagogue-ruler, the *archisunagogos*, or *archon tes sunagoges*, or sometimes more than one, responsible for keeping order in the synagogue (Lk. 13:14) and for acting as a sort of master of ceremonies, by choosing who should preach (Acts 13:15), read the lessons or lead the prayers at a particular service. Since the form of the synagogue service depended simply on tradition, and not, like the Temple service, on Scripture, it was desirable to have someone responsible for seeing that it adhered to the accepted pattern, and the synagogue-ruler fulfilled this role. It is important to realize that he was not normally a teaching elder.[24]

---

[23] There were also local courts of arbitration, in which the three judges were selected *ad hoc* by agreement between the two parties, but not all issues were, of course, suitable for arbitration, which implies two parties, not too seriously estranged. In the Mishnah, courts of arbitration for property disputes are dealt with in Sanhedrin 3:1-4, but the much wider range of issues handled by courts of three are detailed in Sanhedrin 1:1-3. The two kinds of court are contrasted in a *baraita* quoted in Bab. Sanhedrin 6a.

[24] In the *baraita* from Bab. Pesahim 49b, quoted on p.36, the synagogue-rulers are clearly distinguished both from the teaching elders and from the

He might be a founder or benefactor of the synagogue, and he would certainly be its general administrator, if it was used for other purposes than worship, as it often was. But worship remained its main purpose, as is shown by its alternative name *proseuche*, place of prayer (favoured by Josephus and Philo), by its occasional name *sabbateion*, building for use on the sabbath, and by the explicit statement in the Theodotus inscription that he 'built the synagogue for the reading of the Law and for the teaching of the Commandments'. This being so, the main responsibilities of the synagogue-ruler would be his liturgical responsibilities, as the organiser of worship. The synagogue service was very much a lay activity. Any adult male Jew, who was capable of it, might be called upon to read the Hebrew Scriptures, supply the Aramaic translation or recite the standard prayers, though a teaching elder, if present, would normally be called upon to expound what had been read. The synagogue-ruler would, in each case, decide whom to ask.

Since the synagogue-ruler had duties to the synagogue as a congregation, it is not certain that his name originally related to the synagogue-building, but, as each congregation strove to provide itself with a building, the connection became intimate, and his responsibilities towards the building became an inseparable part of his task. This development had evidently occurred by the first century AD, when the New Testament and other evidence show synagogue buildings as normal.

The synagogue had also an attendant, or servant, called in Hebrew *hazzan* and in Greek *huperetes*, who brought out the

---

rulers of the community, and are subordinated to them both. J.T. Burtchaell assumes that the synagogue-ruler was a teaching elder, the chief one in his synagogue, and makes him the forerunner of the monarchical bishop, with the *hazzan* the forerunner of the deacon (*From Synagogue to Church*, ch. 9), but this is convenient rather than convincing. For the actual evidence we have about synagogue-rulers, see L.E. Levine, *The Ancient Synagogue*, pp.390-402.

Scripture-rolls for the reading of the lessons (Lk. 4:20) and had other limited responsibilities. It is stated in the Tosephta, a rabbinical compilation only less ancient than the Mishnah, that he blew a trumpet to announce the beginning of sabbaths and festivals (Tos. Sukkah 4:12), and in the Mishnah itself that it was he who administered sentences of scourging (Makkoth 3:12f).

The way the various office-holders of a Jewish community ranked in the estimation of their fellows is clearly brought out in another Talmudic *baraita*. It runs:

> Let a man always sell all he has and marry the daughter of a scholar (i.e. of a teaching elder). If he does not find the daughter of a scholar, let him marry the daughter of one of the great men of the generation (i.e. the rulers of the community). If he does not find the daughter of one of the great men of the generation, let him marry the daughter of the ruler of synagogues. If he does not find the daughter of the ruler of synagogues, let him marry the daughter of a charity treasurer. If he does not find the daughter of a charity treasurer, let him marry the daughter of an elementary school-teacher, but let him not marry the daughter of one of the 'people of the land' ... (Bab. Pesahim 49b).[25]

Charity treasurers are not actually mentioned in the New Testament, but are mentioned as a well-established institution in the Mishnah (Demai 3:1; Kiddushin 4:5). A *baraita* states that each town should have three – two to collect funds and three to distribute them (Bab. Baba Bathra 8b). Of the other office-holders, it will be seen that the teaching elder ranks first,

---

[25] The 'people of the land' is a name applied in the rabbinical literature to those Jews who were ignorant or neglectful of the Law or of the rabbinical interpretation of it, and who failed to observe the rules of tithing and ceremonial cleanness. The plural 'ruler of synagogues' is curious, but may mean that, just as a synagogue might have more than one ruler (Mk. 5:22; Acts 13:15), so more than one synagogue might have the same ruler.

the community-ruler second and the synagogue-ruler third. The *hazzan* is not listed, but the Mishnah ranks him below the school-teacher (Sotah 9:15), which makes him sixth. One may suspect the rabbis of partiality in ranking the teaching elder first, but the clear distinctions of office are unaffected, even if this is so.

The training of a teaching elder was undertaken by one who was already recognised as such. Thus, Saul of Tarsus was trained at the feet of Rabban Gamaliel I (Acts 22:3). Jesus and the Twelve were by comparison unlearned men (Jn. 7:15; Acts 4:13). This did not mean that they had not been pupils of an elementary school-teacher, near the bottom of the above hierarchy of office-holders, but that they had not been pupils of a teaching elder, at the top of it. The primary subject of higher study was Scripture, but if the teacher was a Pharisee, as most were, his pupils would also be trained in the tradition of the elders, which was partly, indeed, expository of Scripture, but was partly also supplementary to it. When their training was complete, their teacher might ordain them, which he would apparently do by the laying on of hands (Tos. Sanhedrin 1:1)[26]. The Tosephta says in this passage that three must join in the act of ordination, but according to a passage in the Palestinian Talmud it was originally performed by one, the candidate's own teacher; it was later transferred to the national patriarch, who might be joined by two others of his circle, forming a court of three; and this then became the established custom (Jer. Sanhedrin 1:2-4). The transfer to the national patriarch probably took place in the time of Rabban Gamaliel II (AD 80-

---

[26] The term for ordination, *semikhah*, implies this, though explicit references to the laying on of hands are rare, and the term was retained even after the mode of ordination was changed.

120).[27] Having been ordained as an elder, the pupil had a wide scope for his ministry, but he usually settled and earned his living by a trade (cp. Acts 18:3). He was still a layman, not a priest, but a layman who had been trained and set permanently apart.[28] He could now take pupils, and might be invited to teach in his local synagogue, and, according to the *baraita* mentioned earlier, might be appointed by the Sanhedrin as one of the local community judges. By being trained and training others, who would then train others again, he helped to build up and continue a succession of teachers and a tradition of teaching and legal interpretation which would be carried on (cp. Mishnah, Aboth 1:1-18).

There has been much controversy about rabbinical ordination, and some have supposed that it did not begin until after the destruction of the Temple in AD 70. In this case it could not be the source of Christian ordination. However, if the Jewish eldership or presbyterate is confessedly the source of the Christian, if candidates for both were from ancient times formally admitted (as they were), and if the earliest known mode of admission is in both cases ordination by the laying on of hands, the presumption must be that rabbinical ordination goes back some generations earlier than AD 70 and underlies Christian practice.

Objectors argue that Jesus, though not ordained, was allowed to teach in the synagogues and in the courts of the

---

[27] Julius Newman, *Semikhah (Ordination): a Study of its Origin, History and Function in Rabbinic Literature* (Manchester: The University Press, 1950), pp. 13f., 19.

[28] The question which was raised among English Independents (Congregationalists and Baptists) whether a presbyter's ordination is for life, or should be repeated when beginning a new pastorate, can thus be answered from the presbyter's Jewish antecedent. The case of a Christian presbyter like Timothy, who travelled about, ministering in various churches, points to the same conclusion.

Temple; but this proves too much, for Jesus had no formal training either, which admittedly existed in his day. Even in later times, as Newman points out, some distinguished Jewish scholars remained unordained or tried to avoid ordination, and there are other indications that ordination was reckoned less vital than the learning which qualified one for it.[29]

Again, it is objected that Jesus, though not ordained, was addressed, and even claimed the right to be addressed, by the title of 'rabbi' (Matt. 23:8; 26:25,49; Mk. 9:5; 11:21; Jn. 1:38, 49; 3:2; 4:31; 6:25; 9:2; 11:8), which later was formally conferred by ordination (Bab. Sanhedrin 13b). However, this was very much later: it is reported by the Talmud in the name of Rab Ashi (4th – 5th century AD). 'Rabbi' is an honorific title, meaning 'My Lord'; and, since learning mattered even more than ordination, it is easy to believe that the title may have been more freely used at earlier periods, when addressing learned men, especially in the case of a teacher as impressive as Jesus. Jesus was usually addressed as 'Teacher', but on occasion as 'Rabbi', and this is very understandable.

Finally, it is objected that rabbinical ordination was only conferred in Palestine (Bab. Sanhedrin 14a),[30] whereas Christian ordination was from the outset conferred outside (Acts 14:23 etc.). However, the rabbis who state that ordination is thus confined all date from the late second century AD onwards, after the power of ordination had been confined

---

[29] *Semikhah*, pp.24f., 59, 93-7. Thus, a recognised expert, whether ordained or unordained (it is not clear which), is sometimes permitted to decide a case alone, dispensing with the required number of judges. Also, the later confining of ordination to Palestine (see below) could not have occurred if training had not been reckoned more vital than the ordination which it led up to.

[30] See Newman, *Semikhah*, p.6 and ch.7. A different mode of marking the completion of training was consequently adopted outside Palestine, and later in Palestine also, namely proclamation.

to the national patriarch and his court. It was a way of
asserting his authority over the Jews of the Dispersion.
Naturally, the ordinations he conferred were conferred in
Palestine, but at an earlier period, when teachers still ordained
their own pupils, they would have carried the power of
ordination with them wherever they and their pupils might be.

There has also been much discussion of the terminology and
mode of ordination. David Daube usefully distinguishes the
Hebrew words for laying on a hand or hands: *samak*, to lean
(as in offering, consecration or ordination), and *sim* or *shith*, to
place (as in blessing).[31] The other distinctions he makes are
less helpful, and are disputed by Everett Ferguson, who shows
that in early Christianity, partly because the terms are not
distinguished in Greek, ordination is often understood as a
blessing.[32] L.A. Hoffman points out that in the Palestinian
Talmud the normal term for ordain is *manah*, to appoint, and
infers that the Babylonian Talmud is mistaken in interpreting
samak in the Tosephta and *baraitas* as referring to ordination.[33]
This is a bold conjecture, which goes beyond anything that the
Palestinian Talmud says or implies; and if we cannot rely on
the way the Talmuds interpret their sources, even when there is
no clear reason for doubting it, we are indeed at sea. Hoffman
concludes that the mode of rabbinical ordination never was the
laying on of hands. A somewhat similar thesis is argued by O.
Barlea, on equally fragile grounds.[34] He holds that the original

---

[31] *The New Testament and Rabbinic Judaism* (London: Athlone Press,
1956), pp.224-46, 'The Laying on of Hands'.

[32] 'Laying on of Hands: its Significance in Ordination', in *The Journal of
Theological Studies*, NS, vol.26:1 (April 1975), pp.1-12.

[33] 'Jewish Ordination on the Eve of Christianity', in *Studia Liturgica*,
vol.13 (1979), nos.2ff., pp.11-41.

[34] As cited by E.J. Kilmartin, 'Ministry and Ordination in Early
Christianity against a Jewish Background', in *Studia Liturgica*, vol.13 (1979),
nos.2ff., pp.42-69.

mode of rabbinical ordination was not the laying on of hands but installation in a chair. However, these two practices were in no way mutually exclusive, as is shown by the discussion of Moses laying his hands on Joshua and giving him a charge in the old rabbinical commentary on Numbers, roughly contemporary with the Tosephta, where Moses is stated, in addition to this, to have seated Joshua in a chair (Siphre on Numbers 140, on Num. 27:19).

All in all, the laying on of a hand or hands is well established as the original mode of ordaining a Jewish elder, and, that being so, its connection with the similar mode of ordaining a Christian elder is hard to deny.

CHAPTER SIX

FROM JEWISH PRESBYTER
TO CHRISTIAN PRESBYTER-BISHOP

It has often been remarked, with how little explanation the Christian institutional ministry makes its appearance in the New Testament. The apostolate is something of an exception, since we are told how the Twelve are deliberately chosen by our Lord from the wider body of his disciples and are given a charge, but the appointment of the Seven in Acts 6 does not name the office to which they are being appointed, and the appointment of elders in Acts 14 gives no indication of the work which the elders are to do. One is left to infer what the work is from the fact that it is elders, or presbyters, who are being appointed on this occasion, and from references to elders elsewhere.

Traditionally, from Irenaeus onwards (*Against Heresies* 3:12:10), the appointment of the Seven has been regarded as the institution of the Christian diaconate, and, inasmuch as the diaconate is an assistant office, this is not an altogether inappropriate conception. Nevertheless, the Seven are not called deacons, and, if we may judge from the examples of Stephen and Philip, the serving of tables was by no means the extent of their ministry. In later references to the Jerusalem church in Acts, there is frequent mention of presbyters (Acts 11:30; 15:2,4,6,22f; 16:4; 21:18) but no mention of deacons, and what is perhaps particularly significant is that in Acts

11:30 the presbyters have responsibility for poor relief, like the Seven in Acts 6.

On the pattern of Jewish society, one could perhaps regard the Seven as charity treasurers, especially if their number were three not seven; but it needs to be remembered that in New Testament times Christians simply constitute congregations, existing within Jewish (or Gentile) society, and not entire local communities. This is an objection also to David Daube's parallel with the seven delegates of a town, who are entitled to represent the whole town (Jer. Megillah 3:2),[35] for the Christian congregation is not a town; and the Seven are not even chosen to represent the congregation, but rather to represent and take the place of the apostles, who have hitherto dealt with poor relief themselves. Hence, Daube's idea that it is the congregation who lay hands upon the Seven in verse 6, like Israel when they appoint the Levites as their representatives in Numbers 8, is not really appropriate; and it conflicts directly with verse 3 of Acts 6, where the apostles speak of themselves as the ones intending to make the appointment.

In Jewish society, as we have seen, there were six ranks of office-holders in a local community. The assumption, of course, is that it is a well established community, with a synagogue building or buildings, and has provided itself with officers. If a new congregation sprang up within the community, without a synagogue building, and expounding a new interpretation of Judaism, it might at first use the existing building and officers, as far as it conscientiously could, or was permitted to, but it would from the outset require its own teaching elders, who might, indeed, be the cause of its existence. In so far as it needed to make its own provision in

---

[35] See Daube, *The New Testament and Rabbinic Judaism*, as cited in note 31.

other ways (for example, in the distribution of charity among
its members), the teaching elders could be expected to add this
to their duties for the time being, until other officers were
appointed, or until they provided themselves with assistants.
This is perhaps what happened in the early Jerusalem church.

Jesus and his apostles, whatever else they were (and they
were, of course, much else), were teaching elders. This is how
they were perceived in Jewish society, at least by the people in
general, even if not by opponents. Jesus had pupils, like other
Jewish teachers, though his own teacher, as he said, was his
heavenly Father (Jn. 7:14-16; 8:28).[36]　Jesus is constantly
addressed as 'Teacher' and often as 'Rabbi', and never refuses
the titles, but rather encourages them. He refers to his disciples
as 'scribes' and 'sages' (Matt. 13:52; 23:34) and two of them
refer to themselves as 'elders' or 'presbyters' (1 Pet. 5:1; 2 Jn.
1; 3 Jn. 1).[37]　The apostle Paul had been formally trained as an
elder (Acts 22:3), and after he was converted he changed his
teaching but not his teaching method. He still preached in the
synagogues (Acts 9:20; 13:15ff. etc.) and still passed on the
teaching he had received, though now from Christian sources,
committing it to others, who are to commit it to others again, as
true tradition, originating in the Lord Jesus (1 Cor. 11:23; 15:1,
3; 2 Thes. 2:15; 3:6; 2 Tim. 2:2).

---

[36] Did Jesus then start a completely new tradition of teaching? No, but it
was certainly a reformed tradition, appealing to the Old Testament Scriptures
against much in Pharisaic tradition.

[37] 'The elder' in 2 Jn. 1 and 3 Jn. 1 is sometimes identified with a second-
generation Christian named John the Elder who is spoken of, early in the
second century, by Papias (in Eusebius, *Ecclesiastical History* 3:39:4). It
should not be overlooked, however, that in this passage Papias calls the
apostles, John included, by the same name of 'elders'. If he is reflecting the
language of 2 Jn. and 3 Jn., it may as easily be in the latter case that he reflects
it, as in the former. Cp. Acts 21:18, where the 'elders' of Jerusalem seem to
include the apostles. – That the apostles were themselves elders or presbyters is
a fact perceived long ago by Hooker (*Ecclesiastical Polity* 5:78:3f.).

Thus, the eldership was an old Jewish institution, to which Jesus and his apostles could claim to belong. They did not have to create it for their followers, because they already belonged to it themselves. Like other elders, they taught the Old Testament, but taught it according to a fresh, Christian interpretation. And the elders they appointed were to do the same.

The elders who were associated with the apostles at Jerusalem (Acts 11:30; 15:2,4,6,22f; 16:4; 21:18) were probably not all of them elders appointed to the role. Jerusalem was the mother church, and their alternative name in Acts 15:23, 'elder brethren', or senior believers, suggests that they included those (like Joseph Justus, James, our Lord's other brothers and the rest still remaining from the original 120, after the persecution of Acts 8) who had been Christians since Jesus's resurrection or even earlier, who had been associated with the apostles from that stage onwards (Acts 1:13-15, 21-3), and were senior primarily in that sense. This use of the name 'elder' is continued by Papias and Irenaeus,[38] and is a new application of the fourth sense of the term identified on p.33.

The first *appointed* elders were very likely the Seven, who seem from their names all to have been Hellenistic Jews, as was natural from the circumstances of their appointment. Their task was to rule rather than to teach, but Stephen and Philip soon displayed teaching gifts as well. Their training had been short but intensive, and they were selected by the Jerusalem congregation as those of the five thousand church members

---

[38] The collected fragments of Papias and the 'Reliques of the Elders preserved in Irenaeus' can be consulted in the original and in translation in Lightfoot and Harmer, *The Apostolic Fathers* (London: Macmillan, 1891). The second edition, revised by M.W. Holmes (Leicester: Apollos, 1990), is in English only, but includes additional fragments of Papias.

(Acts 4:4) whose faith and wisdom showed they had profited most from the apostles' daily instruction. As the apostles needed such assistants, they were appointed without further delay, and the apostles simply confirmed the congregation's choice, rather than attempting to choose independently, as they might have done in other circumstances.[39] According to 1 Clement 44, they would still have looked for 'the consent of the whole church', however.

This brevity and informality of training might seem an argument against regarding the Seven as presbyters, were it not that in the next instance, where the term 'presbyters' is explicitly used, the circumstances are similar. When the Gentile mission begins, Paul and Barnabas, described in Acts 13:1 as 'prophets and teachers' (names which are also applied to Jesus), are sent out by the church of Antioch on their journey to Cyprus and Asia Minor (modern Turkey), in the course of which they appoint presbyters in every church that they found (Acts 14:23). It is no doubt significant that they do this on their return journey and not on their first visit to plant the churches, but, apart from what they are able to impart on their two visits, the only training which most of these presbyters could have received, at least as Christians, would have been their study of the Scriptures in the intervening period. This was inevitable in the circumstances: afterwards a more extended training was evidently introduced, to avoid the appointment of novices or hypocrites (1 Tim. 3:6; 5:22). But since the Twelve had been so thoroughly trained by Jesus, and Paul at the feet of Rabban Gamaliel, it seems likely that they

---

[39] It is striking that the initiative in the call of the Seven is taken by others, not themselves (contrast 1 Tim. 3:1). As H.J.M. Turner emphasizes in his thought-provoking study *Ordination and Vocation, Yesterday and Today* (Worthing: Churchman, 1990), this has often been the case in the history of Christian ordination.

would from the outset have trained their own pupils with all the thoroughness that circumstances allowed.

Being taken over from Judaism, one would expect the eldership to be present in the church from the beginning, and not to be a later development, and this is what we actually find. Those who assume that the church at first had no institutional ministry to regulate the uncontrolled exercise of charismatic gifts can only do this by ignoring half the evidence and all the probabilities.

In the remainder of the narrative of Acts, we have further references to the presbyters of Jerusalem, who play an important part alongside the apostles and James the Lord's brother in the decisions of the Jerusalem 'council' of Acts 15, and a reference to the presbyters of Ephesus, whom Paul summons to him for his final instructions in Acts 20:17. These are presbyters whom, in accordance with his policy, he had doubtless appointed himself on one of his visits to Ephesus earlier in his second missionary journey. It is here, in verse 28, that we first find presbyters called by their other name of *episkopoi*, bishops or overseers.

Elsewhere in the New Testament, presbyters are referred to in the Pastoral Epistles (1 Tim. 5:17,19; Tit. 1:5), in James 5:14 and in 1 Peter 5:1, and, by their other name of 'bishops', in the Pastoral Epistles again (1 Tim. 3:1f; Tit. 1:7) and in Philippians 1:1. As presbyters they taught, and as bishops they exercised oversight. 'Bishop', being a new name in this connection, apparently transferred from secular use, is not found so regularly.[40] Alternative expressions are *hegoumenos*,

---

[40] *Episkopos* could be a translation of the term *mebakker*, found in the Dead Sea Scrolls, for Qumran has many parallels with primitive Christianity, but the role of the latter figure is not altogether clear. Each Essene community may have had at its head two officers, a priest and a *mebakker*, or 'overseer', probably a Levite (see Geza Vermes, *The Dead Sea Scrolls in English*,

ruler (Heb. 13:17, 24) and *poimen*, shepherd, pastor (Eph.
4:11). In Galatians 6:6 and 1 Thessalonians 5:12 none of the
standard names are used (for whatever reason), but the
activities that the presbyter-bishops perform are merely
described, namely ruling, teaching and admonishing. It is clear
from all these references how widespread the institution of
presbyter-bishop was in the apostolic church. Corinth is the
sole church where there is reason to doubt its existence, and
this may only be because the enthusiastic Corinthian
pneumatics disregarded the presbyter-bishops, not because they
did not exist there.[41]

The conception of presbyters as not only teachers but also
overseers is reflected not simply in their additional title but in
other ways. 1 Timothy 5:17 speaks of the 'presbyters who *rule*
well'. In Acts 20:28f. the presbyters of Ephesus are bidden to
'*Take heed* unto yourselves, and *to all the flock* ... to feed the
church of God'. 1 Peter 5:2,4 bids the presbyters '*tend* the
flock of God which is among you, exercising the *oversight*',
with the promise that they will receive a crown of glory 'when
the *chief Shepherd* shall be manifested'. It needs to be
remembered that in the Old Testament a shepherd is not a

Harmondsworth: Penguin, 1975, pp.18-25). The parallel with the presbyter-
bishop or with the later bishop is in this case far from close (though compare
p.29f.). In the revised edition, however, Vermes takes the view that the priest
was himself the *mebakker*, and the Levite simply his deputy.

[41] Paul's question to the Corinthians in 1 Cor. 6:5 and his reminder to them
in 1 Cor. 16:15f., as well as his call for order to be restored to Corinthian
worship in ch.14, show that he is far from satisfied that there should be no
institutional leadership there. According to 1 Clement 42, which is addressed
to the Corinthian church, and is actually alluding to 1 Cor. 16:15f., the apostles
'appointed their first fruits (i.e. their early converts) to be bishops and
deacons'. This suggests that Paul appointed Stephanas and members of his
family to those offices. If so, the Corinthians were disregarding their bishops
and deacons when 1 Corinthians was written, just as they had later rejected
their bishops when 1 Clement was written.

sentimental figure but a caring *ruler*, like Joshua (Num. 27:16-20) or David (Ps. 78:70-2), in whose footsteps the Messiah is to follow (Ezk. 34:23; 37:24). When Jesus came, and 'saw the multitudes, he was moved with compassion for them, because they were distressed and scattered, as sheep not not having a shepherd' (Matt. 9:36; Mk. 6:34). Mark tells us that his response was to be their Shepherd himself, 'he began to teach them many things'. He thus revealed himself as the 'good Shepherd' (Jn. 10:11), the 'great Shepherd of the sheep' (Heb. 13:20), the 'chief Shepherd' (1 Pet. 5:4), the 'Shepherd and Bishop of their souls' (1 Pet. 2:25). Matthew tells us that his other response was to send out assistant shepherds and bishops from among his followers, beginning with his twelve apostles, whom he sent out to preach (Matt. 9:37-11:1; cp. also Jn. 21:15-17). Their shepherding was in great part evangelism, for they were to bring back the lost sheep and reap the spiritual harvest (Matt. 9:36-8; 10:6), not just to tend the flock. And the presbyters whom the apostles appointed had likewise this role of pastoral oversight, alongside their role as teachers.

At the same time, one must not exaggerate the distinction between the two roles. We have just seen that Jesus and his apostles exercised their role as shepherds chiefly by teaching and preaching. It was no different with the presbyter-bishops whom they appointed, who were to 'feed' the flock, and to protect them against false teaching (Acts 20:28-32). What they were to 'feed' them with was doubtless true teaching. They were to rule the flock, therefore, with the word, and the gospel would nourish the flock in a way that legalistic teaching could never do.

There is good reason to think that the Christian stress on oversight was a fresh development in the role of the Jewish teaching elder. The latter's main work, as we have seen, was to be a judge and a teacher. But judging and ruling had always

been closely connected in Israel, and often in the same person.
There were still varieties of elder who ruled.   The local
community-ruler was an elder.   Those members of the
Sanhedrin who were not chief priests were elders.   But the
local teaching elder had become simply a judge and a teacher,
and the change made by Christianity was to restore to him a
ruling function as well, in the form of pastoral oversight.
Much like the Essene *mebakker*, 'he shall have pity on them, as
a father on his children, and he shall bring them back in all
their distress as a shepherd his flock' (Damascus Document,
CD, 13:9, Fitzmyer's rendering).

The Christian presbyter could still act as a judge. We see
him doing this, alongside the apostles, at the Jerusalem
'council' (or rather appeal-court) of Acts 15.   Also, church
discipline was very active in New Testament times, and though
the church itself was responsible for it, the presbyters doubtless
acted as the church's agents. But Christianity is a gospel and
not a law, and consequently the role of the presbyter as a judge
was bound to decline in importance, tending to be subsumed
under his other two roles of pastor and teacher. These are the
only two roles which are mentioned in the directions about the
choice of suitable persons as presbyter-bishops in the Pastoral
Epistles. Anyone chosen must be suitable to be an 'overseer',
or 'God's steward' (1 Tim. 3:1f; Tit. 1:7), one who can prove
his capacity to take care of the church of God by ruling his own
household well (1 Tim. 3:4f). He must also be suitable to be an
'elder' (Tit. 1:5), and hence 'apt to teach' (1 Tim. 3:2), 'able
both to exhort in the sound teaching and to convict the
gainsayers' (Tit. 1:9).[42] Nothing is said here about judging (or,

---

[42] Calvin's idea, which became traditional in Presbyterianism, that 1 Tim.
5:17 refers also to a second class of elders who rule but do not teach (*Institutes*
4:11:1), is probably a misunderstanding, as reference to 1 Tim. 3:2; Tit. 1:9
indicates; but, if he is right, these may be men who are elders simply as older in

indeed, about the administration of the sacraments, though the 'overseer' would, of course, supervise their administration, whether or not he was at this stage regularly administering them himself).[43]

Roland Allen's famous study of Paul's missionary work, and of his practice of ordination in the course of it, identifies six characteristics of the presbyters whom Paul ordained. (i) They were ordained to work in their congregation of origin; (ii) they were not usually young; (iii) they were not highly trained for their work; (iv) they had the power of training and ordaining others; (v) there was more than one of them to a congregation; (vi) they were self-supporting.[44] In four of these characteristics, there was no change from the Jewish teaching elder, and in the other two (the first and third) the necessities of the situation would have been the cause.

Something which Peter says to the Christian elders of Asia Minor whom he addresses must on no account be overlooked: 'not as lording it over the charge allotted to you, but making

---

years and in the faith, like some of the elders of the Jerusalem church. In pursuance of his interpretation, Calvin also divides the pastor-teachers of Eph. 4:11 into two separate ministries, exercised by different people (*Institutes* 4:3:4), but this is contrary to the Greek construction.

[43] As Hooker points out (*Ecclesiastical Polity* 5:77:1f.), no one may administer divine things without receiving authority from God to do so; but this does not mean that the authority may not be delegated, or that in case of necessity it may not even be dispensed with, for the real minister is God or Christ. Whoever the earthly minister of the sacraments may be, it can only be Christ himself who baptizes with the Spirit (Jn. 1:33) and who imparts his own body and blood. At 'the Lord's table' (1 Cor. 10:21), the host is always the Lord, and the minister (whether apostle, presbyter-bishop or the delegate of either) is at most an assistant.

[44] *Missionary Methods, St. Paul's or Ours?* (2nd edn. reprinted, London: Lutterworth, 1968), chs.6,9. It can hardly pass without mention that all but one of these six characteristics (the fourth) are to be found in the Non-Stipendiary Ministry recently introduced in the Church of England. This shows how easy it is for the Anglican ministry to return to its roots.

yourselves ensamples to the flock' (1 Pet. 5:3). An elder was a senior man entitled to respect. A 'bishop' was an overseer, exercising authority. A presbyter-bishop bore both titles. So he must never forget the example which Jesus set his apostles, showing them that the way of Christian greatness is the way of humility, not to be served but to serve (Mk. 10:42-5; Jn. 13:12-17).

The manner in which presbyter-bishops were appointed was evidently by the laying on of hands. The words *cheirotoneo* and *kathistemi*, used in Acts 14:23 and Titus 1:5, simply mean 'appoint', but the Seven are appointed by the laying on of hands (Acts 6:6), and there are three other examples, all in the Pastoral Epistles.[45] 1 Timothy 5:22 refers generally to the ordination of presbyter-bishops, and possibly deacons, while 1 Timothy 4:14 and 2 Timothy 1:6 both refer to the case of Timothy. The last passage speaks of Paul laying his hands upon Timothy, which would accord with first-century Jewish practice, when teachers still ordained their own pupils; and David Daube is probably right in interpreting 1 Timothy 4:14 as meaning 'the laying on of hands for the presbyterate',[46] which would fit in well with the other passage. To interpret it as meaning the laying on of hands by the presbyterate, as if other presbyters joined Paul in the action, would only accord with second-century Jewish practice, after ordination had been transferred to the national patriarch and his court. To the objection that Timothy was not a local teaching elder but an 'evangelist' (2 Tim. 4:5), the answer is that Timothy was nevertheless a trained pupil of a senior teaching elder, and that this would have been sufficient grounds, in the context of

---

[45] Acts 13:3 is a commissioning of missionaries, for a particular missionary journey, rather than an ordination, so is hardly relevant.

[46] See Daube, *The New Testament and Rabbinic Judaism*, as cited in note 31. This interpretation was earlier proposed by Calvin (*Institutes* 4:3:16).

Jewish practice, for ordaining him. We have no reason to think that the fact that he was engaged in an itinerant ministry, as his master also was, would have made any difference. Philip, the other 'evangelist' named in the New Testament (Acts 21:8), had been ordained among the Seven before engaging in his itinerant work, and the distinction in Ephesians 4:11 between 'evangelists' and 'pastor-teachers' is probably a distinction between preachers who travel as missionaries and those who are locally based, though they may both be presbyters.

Those who ordained presbyter-bishops were in Acts 6 and Acts 14 apostles (themselves 'fellow-elders', 1 Pet. 5:1), though in Acts 14 Paul is joined by Barnabas, one of those 'elder brethren' who were associated with the apostles in their evangelistic work; and others of these were Silas and Apollos, who may also have ordained. Then there were younger associates, ordained by the apostles, Philip the Evangelist, Timothy and probably Titus, who could pass on to others the ordination they had themselves received, as we see two of them doing in the Pastoral Epistles. 1 Clement 44 speaks of the wronged presbyter-bishops of Corinth as having been appointed either by the apostles or afterwards by 'other eminent men'.

One should not ignore the references in 1 Timothy 4:14 and 2 Timothy 1:6 to the 'gift (*charisma*) of God' which was given through the laying on of hands. Though in Timothy's case this was accompanied by prophecy (presumably about his future ministry), it is the ordinary Pauline word for spiritual gifts, which were available to every member of the body of Christ (1 Cor. 12); and though, in the cases of other candidates for ordination, it appears from the Pastoral Epistles that signs of a gift for teaching and oversight were to be looked for before ordination, as qualifications, this does not exclude ordination itself from confirming and increasing those gifts. Unlike the two sacraments, in which the outward sign is accompanied by specific New Testament promises of saving grace, the outward sign is here simply said to have been accompanied by a spiritual gift in the case of Timothy; nevertheless, the fact is a definite encouragement to pray for a similar gift at all other ordinations, and it makes ordination under the New Covenant different in this respect from ordination under the Old Covenant.

CHAPTER SEVEN

FROM PRESBYTER-BISHOPS
TO BISHOP AND PRESBYTERS

The only New Testament precedents for the emergence of the bishop as head over the other presbyters (though doubtless important precedents) were the authority exercised by apostles or their fellow-evangelists on their visits to churches, and the authority regularly exercised by James the Lord's brother in the mother-church of Jerusalem. However, the office of presbyter-bishop itself contained the seeds of the development.

In a Jewish community or Jewish synagogue there was frequently more than one teaching elder. It is therefore no cause for surprise that, in the same way, the Christian elder of the New Testament more often occurs in the plural than in the singular. Acts 11:30; 15:2,4,6,22f; 16:4; 20:17; Philippians 1:1; James 5:14, provide particularly clear examples of a single Christian congregation or city-group of congregations with a number of elders. In the letters of Ignatius, the presbyters of a city are described as constituting a 'council' or 'college' (*Magnesians* 6; *Trallians* 3). In one significant respect, however, the Christian congregation differed from the Jewish, which was that, when it met for worship, it evidently had no synagogue-ruler to guide proceedings, by deciding who should read, lead in prayer or preach. Worshipping in houses (Acts 2:46; 18:7; Rom. 16:5; 1 Cor. 16:19; Col. 4:15; Philem. 2), and having no synagogue-building, it naturally had no synagogue-ruler either. If all house-church owners had been as able and forceful as Priscilla and Aquila, this might not have mattered much, but presumably they were not. In Corinth, where there was not even an effective eldership either, we know from 1 Corinthians 14 that the result was great disorder. Moreover, where there was an effective eldership, there was still no one apart from the elders themselves to make the decisions, and if there was disagreement between the elders, what then? One obvious answer to this problem would be to choose one of their number to undertake the duties of the synagogue-ruler, in addition to his existing duties. He, from then on, would either lead the service and preach himself, or decide which others, on any particular occasion, should assist him or deputize for him. From the second century onwards, we find this being done by the 'bishop', who has presumably been selected from among the other presbyter-bishops to fill the gap left by the synagogue-ruler.

A second problem which needed an answer was common to Christians and Jews, and related to ordination. According to the Talmud, as we have seen, each Jewish teaching elder originally ordained his own pupils. The Christian teaching elder, i.e. the presbyter-bishop, would presumably have done the same, and we have seen examples of this in the case of Paul ordaining Timothy, and Timothy and Titus ordaining suitable candidates in Ephesus and Crete. However, to be free to ordain candidates without a title (that is, without a determined sphere in which to exercise their ministry), as the rabbis at first were, doubtless created the same problems at that period as it did in the fifth century and more recently.[47] Moreover, a wayward teacher was only a limited problem, provided he could not ordain others, but if he could, the problem might easily get out

---

[47] See canon 6 of the Council of Chalcedon, which forbids the ordination of deacons and presbyters without titles.

of control. It is probably for reasons of these kinds that, about the end of the first or the beginning of the second century AD, we find Judaism concentrating ordination in the hands of the national patriarch. The breach between the church and the synagogue was now well advanced, but we find the church meeting the same problem at the same period in a comparable way. The church's solution was to concentrate ordination in the hands of the 'bishop'.

A third problem is known to us from Christian sources only and is peculiar to Christianity. In Ignatius, as we saw, the right to celebrate the eucharist, or to authorize others to do so, is being confined to the bishop (*Smyrnaeans* 8). Since the same action was not taken in regard to baptism or the ministry of the word,[48] this may have been due to the special place that the eucharist had in church discipline, which was then so active, and which centred on exclusion from, and readmission to, the Lord's table. Certainly by the third century the responsibility for this sort of discipline had been placed in the hands of the bishop,[49] and Ignatius may reflect an early stage of the process. If so, the reason for making the celebration of the eucharist a prerogative of the bishop was to prevent excommunicated people from evading church discipline by setting up their own communion tables. Their eucharists could now be disallowed

---

[48] It is true that in *Smyrnaeans* 8 Ignatius goes on to say that it is not lawful to baptize without the bishop's approval, but nothing is said this time about his personal participation. Since baptism is received only once or not at all, it may well not have been restricted to the same degree as the other sacrament. Tertullian emphasizes that the bishop has the right to baptize (*On Baptism* 17), but Hippolytus apparently describes others as baptizing, even in the bishop's presence (*Apostolic Tradition* 21). This is not unlike the practice of the apostles (see p.69).

[49] See Joseph Bingham, *The Antiquities of the Christian Church* (1708-22) 19:3:1-3.

by the bishop, thus emphasizing their state of excommunication.

If this reconstruction is right, it means that, about the end of the first century AD, in the interests of order and unity, the presbyter-bishops decided that only one of their number in each church should in future perform three functions which had previously been open to them all, namely: the direction of worship, the practice of ordination and the exercise of discipline. Where this was first decided, and whether all three prerogatives were transferred to the bishop at once, is impossible to say with certainty, but the effectiveness of the transfer in each case meant that it was rapidly imitated elsewhere. Jerome's famous statement about Alexandria would imply that the presbyter-bishops there were slower to transfer the prerogative of ordination than elsewhere, but it would not mean more than that; and since our knowledge of the early Egyptian church is so scanty, it is rash to dismiss his statement.[50] Then, when the presbyters were mostly dispersed

---

[50] What Jerome says is this: 'When subsequently (i.e. after the New Testament period) one presbyter was chosen to preside over the rest, this was done to remedy schism and to prevent each individual from rending the church of Christ by drawing it to himself. For even at Alexandria from the time of Mark the Evangelist until the episcopates of Heraclas and Dionysius (in the mid-third century) the presbyters always named as bishop one of their own number chosen by themselves and set in a more exalted position, just as an army elects a general, or as deacons appoint one of themselves whom they know to be diligent and call him archdeacon. For what function, excepting ordination, belongs to a bishop that does not also belong to a presbyter?' (*Epistle 146, To Evangelus*). The danger of disunity, to which Jerome refers, underlies each of the three problems which were suggested in the text as the likely causes of the emergence of the monarchical bishop. Jerome was writing in the late fourth or early fifth century. For further evidence about the Egyptian church, supportive of Jerome's, see H. Chadwick, 'Episcopacy in the Second Century' (in M.A.C. Warren, ed., *The Office of a Bishop*, London: CBRP, 1948), pp.19-21. According to Jerome's older contemporary Ambrosiaster (*Commentaries on the 13 Epistles of St. Paul*, on Eph. 4:11f.), it

from the bishop's church to the outlying parishes, after the conversion of the Roman Empire, they necessarily regained some of their rights in the direction of worship and the exercise of discipline, but not in the practice of ordination.

The evolution of the sole bishop, which we have described, would have been encouraged by other considerations. The death of the apostles in the course of the first century would have left gaps of various kinds. As eyewitnesses of Christ and bearers of revelation, they would have been replaced by the New Testament writings. As missionaries, they would have been replaced by younger missionaries. But as overseers of missionary congregations, they needed a bishop to replace them. Moreover, some of the younger missionaries would have been elders who had assisted, and when necessary represented, the apostles in their lifetime, and would still have been held in the same respect after their death. Such apostolic men would have been natural candidates for the evolving role of bishop, and Eusebius is probably not mistaken in saying that they succeeded to it (*Ecclesiastical History* 3:4 and 3:37). And then there was the precedent of James the Lord's brother at Jerusalem. So, even without an apostle setting the example of consecrating bishops, as Lightfoot thought likely in the case of St. John, the development is quite explicable.

We have hitherto said little, however, of the two great tasks with which the presbyter-bishop began, those of teaching and pastoral oversight. These the bishop and presbyter, when

---

was at first the most senior presbyter who became bishop, but afterwards the presbyters elected the most suitable of their number. Later still, of course, the choice of candidates ceased to be confined to presbyters. At Rome, to judge from the firm language of Hippolytus, the presbyters' choice required the agreement of the laity: he speaks of the bishop as 'chosen by all the people' (*Apostolic Tradition* 2). Cp. Acts 6:3; 1 Clement 44, with regard to the appointment of presbyter-bishops.

separated into two offices, both retained, each in his
increasingly distinct sphere.[51]   Pastoral oversight continued to
include the supervision of the administration of the sacraments,
but the celebration of the eucharist came to be more and more
regarded as a personal prerogative of bishops and presbyters,
both now often described as priests.[52]   The deacon became for
a while the assistant in pastoral work to the bishop[53] (hence,
perhaps, the later 'archdeacon', though in the passage just
quoted the term is differently explained by Jerome); but after
the dispersal of the presbyters to the parishes the deacon
reverted in time to being the assistant of the presbyter.

The teaching role of bishops and presbyters was greatly
emphasised in the early centuries, and one interesting link with
the Jewish teaching elder is that bishop and presbyter both
often taught seated in a chair. It is from this custom that we
derive the bishop's throne, that is, his teaching chair. The New
Testament speaks of the scribes and Pharisees sitting on
Moses' seat, and loving the chief seats in the synagogues
(Matt. 23:2, 6), and it seems from verse 3 of the chapter that
they sat there to teach. One of the midrashim uses the phrase

---

[51] P.F. Bradshaw says that the prayer for the consecration of bishops in
Hippolytus makes no 'reference to the prophetic/teaching ministry'
(*Ordination Rites of the Ancient Churches of East and West*, New York:
Pueblo, 1990, p.47). This is to ignore the phrase 'to feed thy holy flock',
which is the first task mentioned in Hippolytus's prayer (*Apostolic Tradition*
3), and which no doubt means, as in the New Testament, to feed them with the
word of God. Elsewhere in his useful collection, Bradshaw shows how
prominent the task of teaching is in later Eastern prayers for the consecration of
bishops (pp. 245-7). There is also repeated emphasis on the bishop's role as a
teacher in the third-century Syrian Didascalia.

[52] This description begins with Tertullian and Hippolytus, at the end of the
second and beginning of the third century (see note 16 on p.26), though a
parallel between the Christian ministry and the Jewish, as having exclusive
prerogatives, is drawn as early as 1 Clement 40-44.

[53] Hippolytus says that the deacon is ordained 'to the service of the bishop,
to do what is ordered by him' (*Apostolic Tradition* 8).

'like a chair of Moses' as a familiar standard of comparison: it was evidently a large chair with arms used by the heads of the rabbinical schools (Pesikta 7b, quoted by Strack-Billerbeck, *ad loc.*). Among the early Fathers, Irenaeus says explicitly that 'the seat is a symbol of teaching' (*Demonstration* 2); Clement of Alexandria speaks allusively of presbyters sitting in the 'chief seat' (*Stromata* 6:13), and Origen, more literally, of both bishops and presbyters doing so (*Commentary on Matthew* 16:22); while Tertullian says that in those churches which are of apostolic foundation 'the very chairs of the apostles still preside in their places' (*On Prescription* 36), though now, no doubt, occupied by the bishop. A later text, the Canons of Hippolytus, which dates from the first half of the fourth century, speaks of the 'sitting on the seat' as what distinguishes the ordination of a bishop from that of a presbyter (Canon 4).

The bishop has two other striking links with the Jewish teaching elder. His second link is that he is consecrated by three existing bishops. Hippolytus speaks only of his being consecrated by a plurality of bishops (*Apostolic Tradition* 2), but canon 4 of the Council of Nicaea (AD 325) says 'three at least'. The Apostolic Constitutions, later in the fourth century, fixes the number at three (bk. 8, sect. 4), though the first of the related Apostolic Canons, perhaps influenced by the biblical rule about witnesses (Deut. 17:6; 19:15; Matt. 18:16; 2 Cor. 13:1; 1 Tim. 5:19), says 'two or three'. Although there is a little flexibility here, it is hard not to connect the number with the number who laid hands on a Jewish teaching elder, after ordination was transferred to the national patriarch, at the end of the first or beginning of the second century AD. It thereafter became increasingly the custom for the patriarch, when he laid hands on the candidate, to be assisted by two others, thus forming a court of three, who could decide by majority vote, if necessary, that the candidate was suitable, before going on to ordain him. Similarly, the Christian bishop, although he was chosen by the presbyters and laity of his own church, needed other bishops to consecrate him, and the appropriate number (no doubt significantly) was judged to be three.

The third link is that the bishops of those churches which are of apostolic foundation are believed by the early Fathers to hand down the 'apostolic tradition' of teaching (Irenaeus, *Against Heresies* 3:3-5). This is another form of the argument used by Tertullian about the apostles' chairs; and indeed, in chs. 20f., 27f., 32 of his treatise *On Prescription*, Tertullian presents the argument in Irenaeus's form. Hence, just as the Jewish elder passed on a tradition of teaching, so does the Christian bishop, and, in the case of the bishop, the tradition is derived from the very apostles of the Lord. As we saw earlier (p.44), the apostle Paul claimed to pass on a tradition derived from the Lord himself; the bishops, similarly, claimed to pass on a tradition derived from the apostles. As long as it remained uncorrupted, this tradition was identical in substance with the gospel message written down in the New Testament. And here is the oldest conception of the apostolic succession of bishops: they were a succession of teachers, who handed on the apostolic message.[54] Continuity of ordination may be implied, and continuity of local appointment certainly is, but the emphasis is on continuity of teaching.

It is quite possible that originally these three links connected the Jewish teaching elder with the Christian *presbyter*-bishop, and that the Christian bishop inherited the links from him, though in a way that is now obscure. In the

---

[54] See R.P.C. Hanson, *Tradition in the Early Church* (London: SCM, 1962), pp.157-68. For the likelihood that Irenaeus and Tertullian were anticipated in this line of thought by Hegesippus, of whose book only fragments remain, see C.H. Turner's article 'Apostolic Succession' in H.B. Swete's volume cited in note 12 on p.23.

case of the teaching chair, which the Fathers at first associate with presbyters as well as bishops, there is evidence of this. Be this as it may, the links clearly exist, and in subsequent Christian history it is the bishop who chiefly displays them.

CHAPTER EIGHT

THE DEACON

We have not, up to now, said much about deacons. If the Seven were not actually deacons, the only New Testament references to them are probably Romans 16:1; Philippians 1:1, and 1 Timothy 3, which speak of deacons at Cenchreae, Philippi and Ephesus, all of them churches founded or visited by Paul.[55] 1 Clement 42, already twice quoted, tells us that the apostles appointed the first deacons, as is on every account likely, though 1 Timothy 3 envisages Timothy (as a presbyter-bishop or apostle's representative) appointing others. Although the New Testament references to deacons are so few, this is one of the matters on which the writings of the Apostolic Fathers help to confirm the apparent meaning and implications of New Testament language. In three of the passages mentioned (Phil. 1:1; 1 Tim. 3 and 1 Clem. 42), and also in Didache 15 and Epistle of Polycarp 5, deacons are five times named alongside presbyter-bishops, and in second place to them, and are evidently their assistants, as the name *diakonos* (servant, helper) implies. The deacon is, of course, a servant to the church and to Christ, like other Christians, but in his case, he is this by being a servant to the presbyter-bishops. Ignatius's favourite name for the deacons, 'my fellow-slaves'

---

[55] His visit to Cenchreae is mentioned in Acts 18:18. That 1 Tim. 3 refers to Ephesus is clear from 1 Tim. 1:3. I am assuming that Rom. 16:1 refers to a female deacon, and that 1 Tim. 3:11 does the same, though this is not, of course, certain.

(*Ephesians* 2, *Magnesians* 2, *Philadelphians* 4, *Smyrnaeans* 12), implies the same thing, and in the second of these passages Ignatius explains that they are 'subject to the bishop...and to the presbytery'.

Though the basic meaning of *diakonos* is servant or helper, it is sometimes in the English Bible translated 'minister', and J.N. Collins, in his important book *Diakonia: Re-interpreting the Ancient Sources*, has emphasised that 'minister', in the sense of communicator, is included in the meaning of the Greek term. Ignatius, when he says that deacons are not simply 'deacons of meats and drinks' but 'deacons of the mysteries of Jesus Christ' (*Trallians* 2), brings out this implication, so perhaps the title might most happily be rendered '*ministerial* assistant'.

The lists, in 1 Timothy 3, of qualifications needed for the two offices of presbyter-bishop and deacon are very similar. They cover character, ability and reputation, and extend even to qualifications for the exercise of a measure of oversight by deacons (verse 12, cp. verse 4f.), so it is no doubt a significant exception that aptitude to teach is not required of candidates for the diaconate, though not of course excluded. Their essential spiritual gift would be that of *antilempseis*, helps or helpful deeds (1 Cor. 12:28; cp. Rom. 16:2). Helping other ministers is a most honourable task, not a degrading one, which is why candidates are ordained to perform it. The way deacons are singled out in Philippians 1:1 and 1 Timothy 3 implies, likewise, that their office is a very distinguished one, as 1 Timothy 3:13 indeed states.

It was not until the fourth century or later that the diaconate became in the West just a first step to the presbyterate (which it did not become, to the same degree, in the East),[56] so it appears

---

[56] See Gregory Dix in K.E. Kirk, ed., *The Apostolic Ministry*, p.283f.

that the diaconate was instituted primarily to assist the presbyter-bishops, and to do so in other matters than the ministry of the word. Like the Seven, who were appointed as presbyter-bishops to save the apostles becoming preoccupied with the distribution of charity, in due course the deacons were appointed, to save the presbyter-bishops from becoming preoccupied with such matters either.[57] We need not infer that either the apostles or the presbyter-bishops wanted to avoid charity work altogether, which it seems they did not, but without assistants they could become preoccupied with it, to the detriment of the ministry of the word and prayer. (Incidentally, the linking of prayer with the ministry of the word by the apostles in Acts 6:2-4 is in harmony with the prominent place of prayer both in the ministry of Jesus and in the epistles of Paul.)

The primary way deacons could assist, then, was in charitable work, and thus at Rome about AD 150 Hermas speaks of their duty of relieving widows and orphans (*Shepherd*: Similitude 9:26). However, this does not mean that it was not their task to assist in other ways too, including liturgical ways, and at the same period and place we find them distributing the elements at the bishop's celebration of holy communion (Justin Martyr, *First Apology* 65,67). Indeed, nearly half a century earlier, at Antioch, we apparently find them doing the same thing, when Ignatius says that deacons do not minister mere food and drink but the mysteries of Jesus Christ (*Trallians* 2). In Hippolytus also the deacon has duties of both kinds (*Apostolic Tradition* 4,8,21f.,34).

---

[57] This was not quite the end of the process. By the early third century, the subdeacon had been created, 'in order that he may obey the deacons' (Hippolytus, *Apostolic Tradition* 13).

Whether there were at first female deacons as well as male has been much discussed. Lightfoot was strongly of the opinion that there were, and so were the distinguished contributors to the Ryle report *The Ministry of Women* (London: SPCK, 1919).[58] According to this view, female deacons are referred to in Romans 16:1f; 1 Timothy 3:11; Pliny the Younger, *Letter 10:96, to Trajan*; Syrian Didascalia 16; but it is a permanent diaconate that they exercise, the diaconate not having become simply a first step to the presbyterate before the fourth-century West. What is certain is that in ancient times there are no female elders or presbyters. This is a modern phenomenon, of which the New Testament and the early church know nothing. The seniority exercised by women in biblical times and biblical thinking is well summed up by the Pastoral Epistles: it relates to children and younger women, and perhaps to household servants, but not otherwise to men (1 Tim. 2:11-15; 5:14; Tit 2:4f). For the Fathers, this settled the matter.

The Christian deacon was probably a new institution. There was a certain parallel with the attendant (*hazzan* or *huperetes*) of the synagogue, and *diakonos* has the same meaning as *huperetes*, namely, servant or assistant. Nevertheless, it is not the same name. Another difference is that there was normally a single *hazzan* to a synagogue, but a plurality of deacons to an early Christian congregation (Phil. 1:1; Ignatius, *Magnesians* 6, 13, *Trallians* 2f.,7, *Philadelphians* proem, 4,7, *Smyrnaeans* 8, 12, *Polycarp* 6; Polycarp, *Epistle* 5; Justin Martyr, *First*

---

[58] See also A. Kalsbach, *Die Altkirkliche Einrichtung der Diakonissen bis zu ihrem Erlöschen* (Freiburg im Breisgau: Herder, 1926). For the contrary view, see A.G. Martimort, *Deaconesses: an Historical Study* (ET, San Francisco: Ignatius Press, 1986).

Apology 65,67).[59] Moreover, the *hazzan* was the assistant of
the synagogue-ruler rather than of the teaching elder, and
Christianity had dispensed with the synagogue-ruler, so
inevitably it had dispensed with his assistant as well. In so far
as it had similar needs to meet, compared with Judaism,
Christianity made independent provisions to meet them, with
the single exception of the elder or presbyter. He was the all-
important office-holder with which Christianity began, and in
his case his name as well as his office continued to bear
witness to his Jewish origin.

---

[59] Even in Hippolytus, contrary to what is sometimes supposed, we do not
find a sole deacon assisting the bishop, in the way that the *hazzan* assisted the
synagogue-ruler. In Hippolytus also there is a plurality of deacons to assist the
bishop (*Apostolic Tradition* 4, 21f, 34). The change in Hippolytus is that they
are assisting just the bishop and not also the presbyters, as in Ignatius
(*Magnesians* 2).

CHAPTER NINE

THE ORDAINED MINISTRY AND THE SACRAMENTS

The importance of the sacraments of baptism and holy communion as means of grace, on which the New Testament leaves us in no doubt, makes it all the more surprising that only such general indications are given there of who is to administer them. We referred earlier to the lack of evidence that the apostles or presbyter-bishops were accustomed to administer them in New Testament times, but the subject requires fuller consideration.

The command to administer the sacraments is indeed given in the first instance to the twelve apostles (Matt. 28:16-20; Lk. 22:19; 1 Cor. 11:23-5), and we know of a small number of people at Corinth who were baptized by the hands of the apostle Paul (1 Cor. 1:13-17). However, in telling us this, Paul also tells us that such was not his normal practice, and he goes so far as to say that Christ sent him not to baptize but to preach the gospel. Light is thrown on this astonishing statement by the practice of Peter, who was one of the Twelve, and who in Acts 2:38 commands his converts to be baptized, but in Acts 10:46-8, at the conversion of Cornelius and his household, commits the baptizing of them to others. It seems, then, that the apostles understood Christ's command to baptize as a command to see that converts were baptized, but not necessarily, or even normally, to do the baptizing themselves. This practice, and this use of language, is further illustrated by

John 4:1-3, where Jesus himself is said to baptize converts, but it is then explained that the work of baptizing was actually done by his disciples.

The question now arises, whether the sacrament of holy communion is a similar case? Here too Jesus gave a command to the apostles, 'Do this in remembrance of me'. The case differs in that here Jesus set an example, by celebrating the sacrament, on the first and last occasion that it was administered in his lifetime, himself. On the other hand, there is not a single recorded instance of the apostles following his example, and themselves acting as celebrant, whereas they did, at least occasionally, baptize. It is true that Paul is once said, when at Troas, to have broken the bread (Acts 20:11), but the breaking of the bread seems always to be thought of as a joint act (verse 7; also Acts 2:42, 46; 1 Cor. 10:16), so this does not necessarily mean that he led the service, which was perhaps led by the local ministry, with him as the preacher. Did the apostles, then, commit to others the administration of this sacrament also? One notes that the additional commands given by Jesus at his own celebration (Matt. 26:26-8; Mk. 14:22) apply to all communicants alike. In harmony with this, Paul speaks of the same people, 'we' or 'you', receiving communion and performing the dominical acts (1 Cor. 10:16f; 11:25). Moreover, his emphasis that the Lord Jesus is still the host at his own table (1 Cor. 10:21f.) discourages the idea that any other minister can take his place: whoever performs the dominical acts will only be an assistant, not a substitute, and would therefore not need to be an apostle, but simply a Christian capable of carrying out the Lord's institution in a reliable way.

Let us consider for a moment the alternative possibility: let us suppose that the way our Lord personally officiated at the Last Supper means that holy communion is different from baptism, in that the task of celebrating it should always be confined to people of particular authority in the church – in the first instance the apostles, and after them the presbyter-bishops, from whom the bishops and presbyters of later times have inherited the prerogative.   Needless to say, this is how Christians have often viewed the matter. In that case, the fact that the New Testament does not once record an apostle or presbyter-bishop acting as celebrant is simply an argument from silence, of no real significance. Also, the celebrant, because of his importance, is to be thought of as an actual representative of the Lord, entitled to take his place at the Lord's table. Neither of these contentions is very easy to accept. Again, on this understanding it is hard to see how the Pastoral Epistles could have dealt with the duties of presbyter-bishops without mentioning this important prerogative of theirs. Nor would one anticipate that, in the primitive period, one would find prophets, confessors and even other laymen celebrating communion, as one apparently does (Didache 10; Hippolytus, *Apostolic Tradition 9*; Tertullian, *Exhortation to Chastity 7*). And when the role of presbyter-bishop becomes two separate roles, one would expect Ignatius either to confine what has previously been the prerogative of presbyter-bishops to the bishop alone, or else to specify that the sole alternatives are presbyters. The language he in fact uses, 'the bishop or one to whom he shall have committed it' (*Smyrnaeans 8*), seems to reflect a background where the eucharist has hitherto been celebrated by the presbyter-bishop or one to whom he has committed it, which is no different from the apostolic practice in regard to the other sacrament.

By the end of the second century, it was already becoming unusual for anyone except a bishop or presbyter to celebrate communion. Tertullian says that 'we take the sacrament of the eucharist ... from the hand of none but the presidents' (*De*

Corona 3), doubtless meaning by the presidents, as in other early Western writers, 'the presbyters that rule/preside over the church' (Hermas, *The Shepherd*, Vision 2:4), including 'the president of the brethren', i.e. the bishop, who celebrates communion in Justin Martyr, *First Apology*, 65, 67. But it is significant that Tertullian, when he tells us of this restriction, is listing Christian customs which depend on tradition and not on the New Testament. His full statement is 'We take the sacrament of the eucharist, which was enjoined by the Lord both at a mealtime and upon all, even in gatherings before daybreak and from the hand of none but the presidents'. He evidently holds that, at the Last Supper, the command to celebrate communion was laid by the Lord upon all Christians, and that only later did the custom of confining it to the presidents arise. This explains why he elsewhere maintains that, in exceptional circumstances, a layman may still 'offer', i.e. celebrate communion (*Exhortation to Chastity* 7).

Turning more directly, now, to the original presbyter-bishops, we note that, in the lists of qualifications for this office, the New Testament states that they must be apt to teach and be able to exercise pastoral rule (1 Tim. 3:2,4f; Tit. 1:9). The first of these requirements simply continues what was required of the Jewish teaching presbyter or elder, but the second is added to it, in conformity with the Christian presbyter's additional title of bishop or overseer. Remarkably enough, however, nothing is said about the leading of prayers or the administration of either sacrament. One recalls that, in the Jewish synagogue-service, any suitable male member of the congregation could be invited to lead in prayer, and 1 Timothy 2:8 seems to reflect a similar practice among Christians (cf. also 1 Cor. 14:14-16). So the presbyter-bishop, in his pastoral oversight of the congregation, could invite a suitable layman to perform this role, or he could of course, on occasion, perform it himself. But what about the administration of the sacraments?

The Jewish teaching elder had no responsibility for the administration of sacred ceremonies: this was rather the responsibility of priests. So did the teaching elder's Christian successor have any such responsibility either? It is certainly not a further task which is explicitly laid upon him in the Epistles to Timothy and Titus, in the way that pastoral oversight is. The matter is passed over in silence. So either the presbyter-bishops are not intended to administer the sacraments at all, or, in their role of overseers, they have general responsibility, like the apostles, for seeing that the sacraments are duly administered, whether or not, or to whatever extent, they administer the sacraments themselves.

Among the Jews, as was said above, the administration of sacred ceremonies was the responsibility of priests. They officiated both at sacrifices and at cleansing rites (Lev. 1-7, 12-15, etc.). The holy communion, in its instituted symbolism, is not the offering of a sacrifice, but it is a feast upon a sacrifice – the sacrifice of Christ (1 Cor. 10:14-22). Baptism is a variety of cleansing rite (Jn. 3:25; Heb. 6:2; 10:22), though the defilement that it cleanses away is sin. It is noteworthy that John the Baptist, who was of priestly descent (Lk. 1:5-66; cp. Jn. 1:19), seems constantly to have administered baptism in person. The contrast between his practice and that of our Lord and his apostles is striking. This could perhaps be accounted for by the fact that, under the New Covenant, priesthood is extended to all believers (1 Pet. 2:5,9; Rev. 1:6; 5:10; 20:6), which would mean that all Christians are in principle qualified to administer the sacraments. Their right to do so on any normal occasion, however, would depend on being invited to fulfil this role, either by an apostle, to whom the sacraments were originally entrusted, or by a presbyter-bishop, charged with the pastoral oversight of a congregation.

When, from the end of the second century, the ordained ministry came to be thought of as, in a special sense, priestly, the administration of both sacraments naturally began to be thought of as peculiarly theirs.   But this was a later development.   Again, when, at the Reformation, it became common for the sacraments to be defined as symbolical words, this carried the consequence that those who had special responsibility for the ministry of the word had special responsibility for the ministry of the sacraments also. From the point of view of biblical theology, the Reformers' definition of sacraments has much to be said for it, but since the ministry of the word is not an exclusive prerogative of the ordained ministry, it follows that the ministry of the sacraments is not an exclusive prerogative of theirs either.   It has been a long-standing Christian practice, in emergency cases, for laymen to baptize, and though lay celebration of communion has not been nearly so common in Christian history, it does not appear that in the earliest period it was seen as in principle wrong, provided the layman in question had been invited to perform it by an apostle or presbyter-bishop.

So the ordained ministry of apostles and presbyter-bishops was always involved in the administration of the sacraments, but not necessarily in the direct way that we have been accustomed to think.

CHAPTER TEN

SUBSEQUENT DEVELOPMENTS

In chapters one to nine, we have sought to trace the development of the ordained ministry in the first two centuries of the Christian era, up to the time of Hippolytus early in the third century. Development was not, of course, arrested at that point, so before concluding we will glance at some of the subsequent modifications and changes which link the primitive period with our own.

(i) *The concentration on eucharistic ministry.* We have seen that the celebration of holy communion was early confined to bishops and those they authorised, which by the fourth century meant bishops and presbyters (p.26). We have also seen that the holy communion began early to be spoken of as the offering of sacrifice, which led to those authorised to celebrate it being described by the title of priests (note 16). The ministry of the word was not confined in the same way, nor was baptism, so the celebration of holy communion began to be thought of as the characteristic task of the presbyter or priest, rather than teaching.[60] Though 1 Timothy 5:17 does not

---

[60] The pronouncement of absolution, which the Council of Trent was to link with the celebration of the eucharist as the other main task of the priest (see p.6), appears to be of later origin. It claims the authority of Jn. 20:22f., but probably this does not directly refer to the pronouncement of absolution, but rather to the whole ministry of the word and prayer, of which the pronouncement of absolution is a later and formal expression. Its earliest occurrence is believed to be in the prayer used by third or fourth-century

probably envisage presbyters who do not teach (p.50f., note 42), it certainly envisages presbyters who teach less than others, perhaps because their teaching gifts are inferior; which could be the explanation of the 'silent' bishops referred to by Ignatius in the early second century (*Ephesians* 6; *Philadelphians* 1), who are nevertheless to be respected, and who probably assigned the teaching task on most occasions to others.[61] This would be in the early period referred to by Ambrosiaster, when the most senior presbyter became bishop, not the most able (p.58f., note 50). He could still celebrate holy communion, and the churches were as yet small enough for Justin Martyr and Hippolytus to expect all Christians to come to the bishop's celebration on Sundays (Justin Martyr, *First Apology* 67; Hippolytus, *Apostolic Tradition* 22). Teaching remained prominent in the age of the Fathers, but it was not until the Reformation that teaching was again fully acknowledged as the bishop and presbyter's chief task.

(ii) *The clerical restriction of lay ministries.* This may be evident as early as Hippolytus, who appends to his account of ordination a list of only six lay ministries – confessors, widows, readers, virgins, subdeacons and healers (*Apostolic Tradition* 9-14). The number of laity with a ministry seems already to be limited, contrary to the New Testament picture of the body of Christ. Some of the charismatic gifts may by now have been withdrawn (p.18f.), but this did not mean that any member of the body of Christ was denied a gift or ministry of

---

bishops when readmitting the excommunicate. Its transference to all priests and to their ministry to penitents in general occurred much later.

[61] A different and perhaps complementary explanation of Ignatius's language, derived from Gnosticism, is given by Henry Chadwick in his article 'The Silence of Bishops in Ignatius', in *The Harvard Theological Review*, vol.43 (1950), pp.169-72.

one sort or another. The growth of clericalism nevertheless encouraged the laity too to think of ministry as mainly the preserve of the clergy, and this misconception dies very hard. It was moderated for a time by the prevalence of monasticism, which flourished from the fourth century onwards, but none except those called to celibacy benefited from this influence. Even the Reformation brought only indirect improvement, by encouraging literacy, Bible reading and biblical preaching, leading to a better understanding of personal discipleship. There has, however, been increasing stress on lay ministry since.

(iii) *The dispersal of the plural presbyterate.* The missionary work of the apostles, as the New Testament shows, planted congregations chiefly in towns. A city bishop of the second century was surrounded by a group of presbyters, who could be sent out to evangelise country areas; but by the fourth century, with the conversion of the Roman Empire, it became common for them to be sent to reside permanently in the villages. Thus congregations with a sole presbyterate, instead of the plural presbyterate usual from New Testament times in the towns (p.55), became normal. The sole presbyterate afterwards spread to towns as well, and there something is being done today to restore a plural presbyterate, by reviving an indigenous non-stipendiary ministry, to assist the more mobile full-time ministry. A great deal of the missionary work in the British Isles was done by monks, and for a time the organization of the church was centred more on monasteries than on cathedrals. However, the Roman missionaries brought the familiar diocesan system, and the initiative in building village churches began to be taken by landowners, who appointed a priest and provided for his needs, though the

bishop instituted him (describing his cure as 'mine and thine')
to prevent his being at the landowner's mercy.

(iv) *The regional organization of the episcopate.* The limited
sphere of an ancient bishop's authority was called his parish,
but as wide rural areas became his responsibility the term
'diocese' was borrowed from secular administration. The
calling together of three bishops to consecrate a new bishop
(p.61f.) was an early sign of co-operation between bishops, and
episcopal councils was another. Well before the conversion of
the Roman Empire, the churches of important cities had started
exercising widespread influence, and the organization of the
church followed the general pattern of Roman secular
government. Bishoprics started being grouped into
archbishoprics and patriarchates, and Rome became the most
important see in the West and Byzantium in the East, mainly
because they were the capitals of the Western and Eastern
Roman Empire. Dioceses in England are very large, unlike
dioceses in some other countries, because the evangelization of
the Saxon Heptarchy began with its royal families. After the
Roman Empire and other countries were converted to
Christianity, bishops became dignitaries of the state as well as
the church, and the lay voice in their appointment was often
thereafter that of the monarch.[62]

---

[62] The remarkably general language of Article 23 in the 39 Articles, which
is widely recognised as avoiding any condemnation of non-episcopal
ordination in the reformed churches on the continent, may also be intended to
safeguard the lay voice in ordinations and appointments. Cranmer, in a paper
written in 1540, makes the lay voice, as expressed by the monarch, the chief
voice (*Remains and Letters*, Parker Society, pp.116-17). Hooker, more
cautiously, says that kings do not *make* bishops, or ministers, but only *place*
them (*Ecclesiastical Polity* 8:7:1-7).

(v) *The decline of the diaconate.* Beginning in the fourth century, the diaconate became in the West just a first step to the presbyterate, and not a distinct ministry. The perpetual diaconate has continued in the East to this day, alongside the probationary diaconate; and female deacons, who would in any case not become presbyters, were able to survive for quite a few centuries in the East (in the West they never apparently existed). Today, efforts are being made to revive the perpetual diaconate, as an assistant ministry open both to men and to women.

(vi) *The celibate restriction of women's ministry.* In the first four centuries, three separate ministries for women existed: the enrolled widow (cp. 1 Tim. 5:1-16), the deaconess or woman deacon, and the consecrated virgin. In the fifth to sixth centuries, however, the last started to swallow up the other two, and nuns, now gathered into convents, became the only institutional ministry for women. The dissolution of the monasteries in the sixteenth century meant that even this role for women disappeared, and the Reformers contented themselves with restoring dignity to the calling of wife and mother. It was not until the nineteenth century that institutional ministries for women (and especially single women) were restored, with the revival of the office of deaconess, today widely understood as woman deacon, together with the stipendiary woman parish worker and the woman missionary. Convent life also made a comeback.

(vii) *The celibate restriction of men's ministry.* The early church emphasis on asceticism produced of course male celibates as well as female, and in the eleventh-century West the requirement was introduced that all priests must be celibate (they may still be married men in the East, though bishops may

not).   Old Testament ideas of the ritual cleanness of the
priesthood also played a part.   In the sixteenth century, the
Reformers abolished this requirement.

(viii) *Professionalization.* This was a gradual process. Paul
encouraged presbyters, like their Jewish counterparts, to be
self-supporting (Acts 20:33-5), though he also encouraged
believers to be generous to them (Gal. 6:6; 1 Tim. 5:17). He
does not make a difference in principle between missionaries
and local ministers, so what both Jesus and Paul say about the
labourer being worthy of his hire (Lk. 10:7; 1 Tim. 5:18; cp. 1
Cor. 9:4-14) naturally led to the whole upkeep of the local
ministry being supplied before long in many places, Didache
13 being perhaps the earliest example. Instruction and training
varied a great deal over the years, and in the days of the Roman
Empire was naturally most advanced in intellectual centres like
Alexandria, Antioch and Rome, though afterwards the
monasteries and then the medieval universities became the
centres of Christian education. The new stress on the task of
teaching at the Reformation made education imperative. By
the late Middle Ages, the ordained ministry had become
sufficient of a profession for the minimum age to be reduced in
England to eighteen, and for the minimum age to become in
practice the normal age (the Reformers raised it to twenty-one,
and it was later raised to twenty-three).   By contrast, the
ancient presbyter was a 'senior man', and Timothy's youth (1
Tim. 4:12; 2 Tim. 2:22) was exceptional. We are now
beginning to restore the balance, by ordaining many older
candidates, with experience of life (but are doing it more by
accident than design, one fears).

CHAPTER ELEVEN

LESSONS FOR TODAY

If the above account is, even approximately, how the ordained ministry originated, its origin carries with it important lessons for our understanding of that ministry – lessons which we need to learn anew today.

First, in the Old and New Testaments the 'elders' include all senior believers, not just *appointed* elders; and seniority is entitled to respect and is a qualification for leadership (almost the reverse of present-day ideas).

Secondly, the basic tasks of the ordained bishop and presbyter are teaching (including evangelism) and pastoral care. The bishop is not primarily an administrator, and the presbyter is not primarily a celebrant of the sacraments (vital though the celebration of the sacraments is), but they are both primarily pastors and teachers. Being derived from the Jewish teaching presbyter and from the New Testament presbyter-bishop, it is natural that this should be so.[63] Today we need to call bishops and presbyters back from too great a concentration on other things, to give their main energies to their main responsibilities, in their respective spheres.

Thirdly, and as a consequence of this, the traditional identification of the essential role of the presbyter as the celebrant of holy communion, should be recognised for what it

---

[63] The Prayer Book Ordinal, following the New Testament, lays its emphasis on the same two tasks (though it does not neglect responsibility for the sacraments either).

is, a tradition. It is not the presbyter's essential role in the New Testament. The Christian presbyter-bishop, with his duty of oversight, must always have been responsible for seeing that holy communion was celebrated; to celebrate it himself is a perfectly appropriate task for a bishop or presbyter to perform, as an extension of his ministry of the word; and an early tradition (which deserves respect) has *confined* the task to bishops and presbyters; but the maintenance of this tradition should not be allowed to overshadow their original and chief tasks, of teaching and pastoral care.

Fourthly, since teaching is so important, the Jews regarded the qualifications for teaching as more vital than ordination, which is the solemn commission to exercise them. Ordination was the normal rule, but our Lord himself was one of the exceptions. We too should take a welcoming attitude towards lay and non-episcopal ministries, and recognise learning and orthodoxy in teachers as deserving the greatest honour, in whomsoever they are found. God may commission those whom the church does not! And sometimes it has been lay and non-episcopal ministries which have corrected corruptions that have arisen in episcopal ministry.

Fifthly, though it cannot be proved that the first bishops were consecrated by the apostles, many of the first presbyter-bishops certainly were. The link between apostle and bishop is therefore the presbyter-bishop, not the presbyter: it is an episcopal link. And the presbyter-bishop would have handed down the apostolic tradition of gospel teaching, and the continuity of apostolic commissioning, as surely as any other bishop would have done.

Sixthly, the presbyter-bishop and his successors, the bishop and presbyter, are not in competition with the every-member ministry of the church brought about at Pentecost, but are a necessary complement to it, ensuring that it never lacks the

regular teaching and pastoral oversight that are essential to its
real fruitfulness. The laity also have spiritual gifts, but this
does not mean that they have no need of the spiritual gifts
exercised by the ordained ministry: they have great need of
them.

Seventhly, the sacerdotal conception of the presbyterate (as
distinguished from the priesthood of believers and the priestly
duty to teach) is connected with the eucharistic conception of
the presbyterate, and is not essential to the office. It is a
development depending upon a particular view of the holy
communion, as the offering of a sacrifice, which is not
prominent in the New Testament. The Anglican term 'priest'
is not sacerdotal, but is a contraction of 'presbyter'.

Eighthly, the revival of the perpetual diaconate, alongside
the present probationary diaconate, would open the office to
new candidates, as not necessarily requiring gifts for teaching,
though not of course excluding them. A case can be made out
from the New Testament and the early church for admitting
women to the diaconate (though not to the presbyterate or
episcopate), and the perpetual dioconate would be the right
sphere for them to exercise the office.[64]

Finally, the elder, or presbyter, goes back to the roots of
biblical religion, in the Old Testament not just the New. The
office has the authority of the whole Bible. It developed and

---

[64] The recent Anglican report *For Such a Time as This* (London: Church
House Publishing, 2001) proposes energetic action in reviving a perpetual
diaconate for men and women, but the General Synod has asked first for a
clarification of the relationship between deacons and readers, who are now as
numerous as the clergy. The reader is an assistant office revived in the
nineteenth century, for which a lay commissioning is given, as anciently in
Hippolytus *(Apostolic Tradition* 11). Lay commissioning is not ordination, and
is not accompanied by imposition of hands, but is a formal way of expressing
the recognition which always needs to be given by the church to spiritual gifts,
if they are to be exercised for the benefit of other Christians.

assumed various forms over the years, but without ever completely changing its character. Before the beginning of the Christian era, it had largely taken over from the priests and Levites their instituted responsibility for the ministry of the word. Our Lord and his apostles were elders, who embraced this special responsibility, and they transmitted the office they had inherited to their first disciples, bidding them exercise it in a spirit not of pride but of service, following Jesus's own example. There has been further development since, but the bishop and presbyter of today are both elders: let them honour in their own lives the ministry they have received, and transmit it unimpaired and undistorted to the generations that shall follow, till the Lord comes again. May he come soon!

BIBLIOGRAPHY OF MODERN WORKS
CITED OR CONSULTED

J.L. Ainslie, *The Doctrines of Ministerial Order in the Reformed Churches of the Sixteenth and Seventeenth Centuries* (Edinburgh: T. & T. Clark, 1940)

R. Allen, *Missionary Methods, St. Paul's or Ours?* (2nd edn. reprinted, London: Lutterworth, 1968)

P.D.L. Avis, *The Church in the Theology of the Reformers* (London: Marshall Morgan & Scott, 1981)

O. Barlea, as cited by E.J. Kilmartin, 'Ministry and Ordination in Early Christianity against a Jewish Backgroud', in *Studia Liturgica*, vol.13 (1979), nos.2ff., pp.42-69.

P. Beasley-Murray, ed., *Anyone for Ordination? A contribution to the debate on ordination* (Tunbridge Wells: Marc, 1993)

R.T. Beckwith, *Calendar and Chronology, Jewish and Christian* (Arbeiten zur Geschichte des antiken Judentums und des Urchristentums 33, Leiden: Brill, 1996)

J. Bingham, *The Antiquities of the Christian Church* (1708-22)

Book of Common Prayer (1662)

P. Bradshaw, *Liturgical Presidency in the Early Church* (Grove Liturgical Study 36, Bramcote: Grove Books, 1983)

P. Bradshaw, *Ordination Rites of the Ancient Churches of East and West* (New York: Pueblo, 1990)

J.T. Burtchaell, *From Synagogue to Church* (Cambridge University Press, 1992)

J. Calvin, *Institutes of the Christian Religion* (Calvin's last French edition, 1559)

R.A. Campbell, 'The Elders of the Jerusalem Church', in *The Journal of Theological Studies*, NS, vol. 44:2 (Oct. 1993), pp.511-28

R.A. Campbell, *The Elders: Seniority within earliest Christianity* (Edinburgh: T. & T. Clark, 1994)

H. Chadwick, 'Church Leadership in History and Theology' and 'Some Theological and Historical Considerations', in report *Senior Church Appointments* (London: Church House Publishing, 1992), pp.75-89, 89-98

H. Chadwick, *The Early Church* (revised edn., London: Penguin, 1993)

H. Chadwick, 'Episcopacy in the Second Century', in M.A.C. Warren, ed., *The Office of a Bishop* (London: CBRP, 1948)

H. Chadwick, 'The Silence of Bishops in Ignatius', in *The Harvard Theological Review*, vol.43 (1950), pp.169-72

J.N. Collins, *Diakonia: Re-interpreting the Ancient Sources* (New York: OUP, 1990)

Y. Congar, *Priest and Layman* (ET, London: Darton, Longman & Todd, 1967)

T. Cranmer, *Remains and Letters* (Cambridge: Parker Society, 1846)

D. Daube, *The New Testament and Rabbinic Judaism* (London: Athlone Press, 1956)

J. Delorme, ed., *Le ministère et les ministères selon le Nouveau Testament* (Paris: Editions du Seuil, 1974)

G. Dix, 'The Ministry in the Early Church', in K.E. Kirk, ed., *The Apostolic Ministry, q.v.*

Episcopal Ministry (report, London: Church House Publishing, 1990)

A.M. Farrer, 'The Ministry in the New Testament', in K.E. Kirk, ed., *The Apostolic Ministry, q.v.*

For Such a Time as This: a Renewed Diaconate in the Church of England (report, London: Church House Publishing, 2001)

E. Ferguson, 'Laying on of Hands: its Significance in Ordination', in *The Journal of Theological Studies*, NS, vol.26:1 (April 1975), pp.1-12

R.Y.K. Fung, 'Charismatic versus Organized Ministry?' in *The Evangelical Quarterly*, vol.52:4 (Oct. 1980), pp.195-214

R.Y.K. Fung, 'Function or Office?' in *Evengelical Review of Theology*, vol.8 (1984), pp.16-39

J. Godfrey, *The English Parish 600-1300* (London: SPCK, 1969)

R.P.C. Hanson, *Tradition in the Early Church* (London: SCM, 1962)

A. von Harnack, *The Constitution and Law of the Church in the First Two Centuries* (ET, London: Williams & Norgate, 1910)

A. Tindal Hart, *The Country Priest in English History* (London: Country Book Club, 1960)

E. Hatch, *The Organization of the Early Christian Churches* (Bampton Lectures, 3rd ed., London: Rivingtons, 1888)

P. Heath, *The English Parish Clergy on the Eve of the Reformation* (London: Routledge, 1969)

L.A. Hoffman, 'Jewish Ordination on the Eve of Christianity', in *Studia Liturgica*, vol.13 (1979), nos.2ff., pp.11-41

D.R.J. Holloway, *Episcopal Oversight: a Case for Reform* (Latimer Study 48, Oxford: Latimer House, 1994)

R. Hooker, *Of the Laws of Ecclesiastical Polity* (1594-7, 1648, 1662)

T.G. Jalland, 'The Doctrine of the Parity of Ministers', in K.E. Kirk (ed.), *The Apostolic Ministry, q.v.*

J. Jewel, *Works* (Cambridge: Parker Society, 1845-50)

A. Kalsbach, *Die Altkirchliche Einrichtung der Diakonissen bis zu ihrem Erlöschen* (Freiburg im Breisgau: Herder, 1926)

E.J. Kilmartin, see O. Barlea

K.E. Kirk, ed., *The Apostolic Ministry* (London: Hodder & Stoughton, 1946)

H. Kraemer, *A Theology of the Laity* (London: Lutterworth, 1960 reprint)

G.W. Kuhrt, *An Introduction to Christian Ministry* (London: Church House Publishing, 2000)

A. Lemaire, *Les minstères aux origines de l'Eglise* (Paris: Editions du Cerf, 1971)

L.I. Levine, *The Ancient Synagogue* (New Haven: Yale University Press, 2000)

J.B. Lightfoot, *The Christian Ministry* (London: Macmillan, 1901; first published 1868)

Lightfoot and Harmer, eds., *The Apostolic Fathers* (London: Macmillan, 1891, and Leicester: Apollos, 1990)

A.G. Martimort, *Deaconesses: an Historical Study* (ET, San Francisco: Ignatius Press, 1986)

J. Newman, *Semikhah (Ordination): a Study of its Origin, History and Function in Rabbinic Literature* (Manchester University Press, 1950)

R. O'Day, *The English Clergy: the Emergence and Consolidation of a Profession 1558-1642* (Leicester University Press, 1979)

The Position of the Laity in the Church (1902 Convocation report reprinted, Westminster: Church Information Board, 1952)

L.I. Rabinovitz, 'Elder: in the Talmud', in *Encyclopaedia Judaica*

A.M. Ramsey, *The Christian Priest Today* (London: SPCK, 1972)

H. Reviv, *The Elders in Ancient Israel: a Study of a Biblical Institution* (Jerusalem: Magnes Press, 1989)

D.W.B. Robinson, 'Ministry/Service in the Bible', in D. Robarts, ed., *Forward in Faith?* (Enmore: Aquila Books, 1998)

J. Armitage Robinson, ed., *St. Paul's Epistle to the Ephesians* (London: Macmillan, 1903)

A. Russell, *The Clerical Profession* (London: SPCK, 1980)

H.E. Ryle, ed., *The Ministry of Women* (report, London: SPCK, 1919)

C. Schams, *Jewish Scribes in the Second-Temple Period* (Sheffield: JSOT Supplement Series 291, 1998)

E. Schillebeeckx, *The Church with a Human Face* (ET, London: SCM, 1985)

E. Schweizer, *Church Order in the New Testament* (ET, London: SCM, 1961)

H.L. Strack and P. Billerbeck, *Kommentar zum Neuen Testament aus Talmud und Midrasch* (Munich: Beck, 1922-61)

J.R.W. Stott, *One People* (London: Falcon Books, 1969)

E.L. Sukenik, *Ancient Synagogues in Palestine and Greece* (Schweich Lectures, London: British Academy, 1934)

H.B. Swete, ed., *Essays on the Early History of the Church and the Ministry* (London: Macmillan, 1918)

Thirty-nine Articles of Religion (1571)

Trent, Council of, *Decrees and Canons* (1545-63)

C.H. Turner, 'Apostolic Succession', in H.B. Swete, ed., *Essays on the Early History of the Church and the Ministry, q.v.*

H.J.M. Turner, *Ordination and Vocation, Yesterday and Today* (Worthing: Churchman Publishing, 1990)

G. Vermes, *The Dead Sea Scrolls in English* (Harmondsworth/London: Penguin, 2nd ed. 1975, 3rd ed. 1987)

J. Whitgift, *Works* (Cambridge: Parker Society, 1851-3)

INDEXES

1. INDEX OF BIBLICAL REFERENCES

Genesis
25:8   *28*
50:7   *29 n.17*

Exodus
3:16, 18   *28*
18:13-26   *29*

Leviticus
1-7   *73*
4:15   *28*
10:10f.   *30*
12-15   *73*
19:32   *28*

Numbers
8   *43*
11:16-30   *29*
22:4, 7   *29 n.17*
27:16-20   *49*

Deuteronomy
1:9-18   *29*
17:6   *61*
17:8-13   *29*
19:12   *28*
19:15   *61*
21:19f.   *28*
22:15-18   *28*
31:9-13   *28*
33:10   *30*

Joshua
20:4   *28*
24:31   *33*

Judges
2:7   *33*
21:16   *28*

Ruth
4:2, 4, 9, 11   *28*

1 Samuel
4:3   *28*

2 Samuel
3:17   *28*

1 Kings
8:1, 3   *28*
12:6-15   *28*
21:8, 11   *28*

2 Kings
10:1, 5   *28*
23:1   *28*

1 Chronicles
11:3   *28*

2 Chronicles
19:8-11   *29*

Ezra
5:5, 9   *28*

Psalms
78:70-2   *49*
119:100   *29*
148:12   *28*

Proverbs
4:1 *28*
5:1 *28*
17:6 *28*

Ecclesiastes
4:13 *29*

Jeremiah
26:17 *28*
31:13 *28*

Lamentations
1:19 *33*
4:16 *33*

Ezekiel
8:1 *28*
34:23 *49*
37:24 *49*

Malachi
2:6f. *30*

Matthew
7:29 *31*
9-11 *49*
9:36-8 *49*
10:6 *49*
13:52 *44*
15:2 *33*
18:16 *61*
21:23 *33*
23:2 *60*
23:6 *31, 60*
23:8 *39*
23:34 *31 n.19, 34, 44*
26:3, 47 *33*
26:25, 49 *39*
26:26-8 *70*
27:1 *33*
27:3, 12, 20 *33*
28:11f. *33*
28:16-20 *69*

28:19 *25*

Mark
1:21f. *31*
5:22 *36 n.25*
6:34 *49*
8:31 *33*
9:5 *39*
10:42-5 *52*
11:21 *39*
13:9 *34*
14:22 *70*
14:53 *33*
15:1 *33*

Luke
1:5-66 *73*
2:46 *31*
4:20 *36*
5:17 *31*
6:6f. *31*
7:3 *22, 31*
7:3-5 *31*
10:7 *80*
13:14 *34*
22:19 *25, 69*
22:66 *33*

John
1:19 *73*
1:33 *51 n.43*
1:38, 49 *39*
3:2 *39*
3:25 *73*
4:1f. *25*
4:1-3 *70*
4:31 *39*
6:25 *39*
7:14-16 *44*
7:15 *37*
8:28 *44*
9:2 *39*
9:22 *33*
10:11 *49*

11:8 *39*
12:42 *31, 33*
13:12-17 *52*
16:2 *33*
20:22f. *75 n.60*
21:15-17 *49*

Acts of the Apostles *15, 17*
1:13-15, 21-3 *45*
2:17 *28*
2:38 *69*
2:42 *70*
2:46 *55, 70*
4:4 *46*
4:5 *32, 33*
4:8 *33*
4:13 *37*
4:23 *33*
5:21 *29*
6 *43, 53*
6:2-4 *66*
6:3 *43, 58f. n.50*
6:6 *43, 52*
8 *45*
9:20 *44*
10:46-8 *69*
10:48 *25*
11:30 *20, 42f., 45, 55*
13:1 *18, 46*
13:2f. *20 n.10*
13:3 *52 n.45*
13:14-44 *32*
13:15 *34, 36 n.25*
13:15ff. *44*
14 *42, 53*
14:4, 14 *20 n.10*
14:23 *20, 39, 46, 52*
15 *20, 47, 50*
15:2, 4, 6, 22f. *42, 45, 55*
15:21 *32*
15:23 *45*
16:4 *41, 45, 54*
18:3 *38*
18:7 *55*

18:18 *64 n.55*
20 *13, 21*
20:7 *70*
20:11 *70*
20:17 *11, 47, 55*
20:28 *11, 12 n.2, 47*
20:28f. *48*
20:28-32 *49*
20:33-5 *80*
21:8 *53*
21:18 *42, 44 n.37, 45*
22:3 *37, 44*
22:5 *33*
22:19 *34*
23:6-9 *32*
23:14 *33*
25:15 *33*
26:11 *34*

Romans
9:22 *16 n.6*
12 *17*
12:7, 8 *20*
15:18f. *19*
16:1 *64 & n.55*
16:1f. *67*
16:2 *65*
16:5 *55*

1 Corinthians
1:13-17 *25, 69*
6:5 *48 n.41*
9:1 *20 n.10*
9:4-14 *80*
10:14-22 *73*
10:16 *70*
10:16f. *25, 70*
10:21 *51 n.43*
10:21f. *70*
11:23 *44*
11:23-5 *69*
11:24f. *25*
11:25 *25, 70*
12 *17, 53*

12:8, 9   *20*
12:11   *19*
12:28   *19, 20, 65*
14   *17, 48 n.41, 56*
14:1, 3   *19*
14:14-16   *72*
15:1, 3   *44*
15:7   *20 n.10*
16:15f.   *48 n.41*
16:19   *55*

2 Corinthians
8:23   *20 n.10*
12:11f.   *19*
13:1   *61*

Galatians
1:19   *20 n.10*
6:6   *48, 80*

Ephesians
2:20   *19*
3:5   *19*
4:11   *48, 50f. n.42, 53*
4:15f.   *16 n.6*

Philippians
1:1   *11f. & n.2, 17 & n.7, 21, 47, 55,*
   64, 65, 67

Colossians
4:15   *55*

1 Thessalonians
5:12   *48*
5:19f.   *19*

2 Thessalonians
2:15   *44*
3:6   *44*

Pastoral Epistles   *12 n.2, 15, 16, 17,*
   53

1 Timothy
1:3   *25, 64 n.55*
1:18   *17*
2:8   *72*
2:11-15   *67*
3   *12, 13, 64 & n.55, 65*
3:1   *46 n.39*
3:1f.   *47, 50*
3:2   *50 n.42, 72*
3:2-13   *20*
3:4f.   *51, 65, 72*
3:6   *46*
3:11   *67*
3:12   *65*
3:13   *65*
4:1   *17*
4:12   *80*
4:14   *17, 52, 53*
5:1   *28*
5:1-16   *79*
5:14   *67*
5:17   *47, 48, 50f. n.42, 75f., 80*
5:18   *80*
5:19   *12 n.2, 47, 61*
5:22   *46, 52*

2 Timothy
1:6   *52, 53*
1:18   *25*
2:2   *44*
2:22   *80*
4:5   *52*
4:12   *25*

Titus
1:5   *20, 25, 50, 52*
1:5-7   *11*
1:6-9   *20*
1:7   *50*
1:9   *50 & n.42, 72*
2:4f.   *67*

Philemon
2   *55*

Hebrews
2:4 *19*
6:2 *73*
10:22 *73*
11:2 *33*
13:17, 24 *48*
13:20 *49*

James
5:14 *21, 47, 55*

1 Peter
2:5, 9 *73*
2:25 *49*
5:1 *44, 47, 53*
5:1-4 *21*
5:1-5 *28*

5:2 *11, 48*
5:3 *52*
5:4 *48, 49*

2 John
1 *44 & n.37*

3 John
1 *44 & n.37*
9-12 *25*

Revelation
1:6 *73*
4:4 *33*
5:10 *73*
20:6 *73*

2. INTERTESTAMENTAL INDEX

APOCRYPHA

Judith
4:8 *29*
6:14-16 *29*
8:10f. *29*
10:6 *29*

Wisdom
4:8f., 13 *29*
8:10 *29*

Ecclesiasticus
3:29 *30*
6:34 *29, 30*
8:8f. *29, 30*
18:27-9 *30*
25:3-6 *29, 30*
27:11f. *30*

37:22-6 *30*
38:24 – 39:11 *30*

Susanna
5f. *29*
41 *29*
45 *29*
50 *29*

1 Maccabees
7:33 *33*
11:23 *33*
12:6, 35 *29*

2 Maccabees
1:10 *29*

PSEUDEPIGRAPHA

Letter of Aristeas
32 *30*
121f. *30*
184 *30*
310 *30*

318 *30*
321 *30*

Ascension of Isaiah
3:21-31 *18f.*

DEAD SEA SCROLLS *47f., n.40*

Damascus Document

CD, 13:9 *50*

PHILO *34*

Hypothetica

7:13 *30f.*

JOSEPHUS *34*

Antiquities
4:214, 287 *29f.*
12:138 *29*

War
2:570f. *29f.*

THEODOTUS INSCRIPTION *31, 35*

RABBINICAL LITERATURE

Mishnah *31 n.19*
  Demai 3:1 *36*
  Maaser Sheni 5:9 *31 n.18*
  Shabbath 16:8 *31 n.18*
  Nedarim 5:5 *32*
  Sotah 9:15 *37*
  Kiddushin 4:5 *37*
  Sanhedrin 1 *34*
          1:1-3 *34 n.23*
          3:1-4 *34 n.23*
          11:1f. *31 n.18*
  Makkoth 3:12f. *35*
  Aboth 1:1 *33*
          1:1-18 *38*
          5:21 *28*

Tosephta
  Sukkah 4:12 *36*

  Baba Metzia 11:23 *32*
  Sanhedrin 1:1 *37*

Midrashim
  Siphre on Numbers 140 *41*
  Pesikta 7b *60f.*

Palestinian Talmud *40*
  Jer. Megillah 3:2 *43*
  Jer. Sanhedrin 1:2-4 *37, 52*

Babylonian Talmud *40*
  Bab. Pesahim 49b *34 n.24, 36f.*
  Bab. Baba Bathra 8b *36*
  Bab. Sanhedrin 6a *34 n.23*
          13b *39*
          14a *39*
          88b *34, 38*

3. PATRISTIC INDEX

FIRST TO SECOND CENTURY

1 Clement
40-44   *58f. n.50*
42   *12, 25f., 48 n.41, 64*
44   *12, 26 n.16, 45, 58f. n.50*

Didache
10   *26 n.16, 71*

Didache (continued)
11f.   *18*
13   *80*
14   *26 n.16*
15   *12, 18, 64*

SECOND CENTURY

Ignatius   *9f., 12*
   Ephesians 2   *64f.*
      6   *76 & n.61*
   Magnesians 2   *64f., 68 n.59*
      6   *55, 67*
      13   *67*
   Trallians 2   *65, 66*
      2f.   *67*
      3   *55*
      7   *67*
   Philadelphians proem   *67*
      1   *76 & n.61*
      4   *64f., 67*
      7   *67*
   Smyrnaeans 8   *26, 57 & n.48,*
      67, 71
      12   *64f., 67*
   Polycarp 6   *67*

Polycarp
   Epistle 5   *12, 64*

Papias   *44 n.37, 45 & n.38*

SECOND TO THIRD CENTURY

Clement of Alexandria
   Stromata 6:13   *61*
Tertullian
   On Baptism 17   *26 n.16, 57 n.48,*
      60 n.52

Hermas, Shepherd of   *18*
   Vision 2:4   *18, 72*
      3:5   *18*
   Similitude 9:15f.   *18*
      9:26   *66*

Justin Martyr
   Dialogue with Trypho 82   *18*
   First Apology 65   *66, 67f., 72*
      67   *66, 67f., 72, 76*

Hegesippus   *62 n.54*

Irenaeus   *19, 45 & n.38*
   Against Heresies 2:31:2   *19 n.9*
      2:32:4   *19 n.9*
      3:2:2 - 3:4:1   *12*
      3:3-5   *62*
      3:3:4   *9*
      3:12:10   *42*
      4:26:2-5   *12*
      5:6:1   *19 n.9*
   Demonstration 2   *61*

Tertullian (continued)
   On Prescription 20f.   *62*
      27f.   *62*
      32   *62*
      36   *61*

De Corona   Exhortation to Chastity 7
  (on the Soldier's Crown) 3   *71f.*   *26 n.16, 60 n.52, 71, 72*

THIRD CENTURY

Hippolytus   21f.   *66, 68 n.59*
  Apostolic Tradition   22   *76*
      2   *58f. n.50, 61*   34   *66, 68 n.59*
      3   *26 n.16, 60 nn.51, 52*
      4   *66, 68 n.59*   Origen
      8   *26 n.16, 60 n.52f., 66*   Commentary on Matthew 16:22
      9   *26 n.16, 71*   *61*
      9-14 *76, 83n.64*
      13   *66 n.57*   Syrian Didascalia   *60 n.51*
      21   *57 n.48*   16   *67*

FOURTH CENTURY

Eusebius   Canon 4   *61*
  Ecclesiastical History   Ambrosiaster   *24 n.13*
      3:4:3-11   *59*   Commentaries on the 13 Epistles
      3:39:1-7   *59*   of St. Paul, on Eph. 4:11f.
      3:39:4   *44 n.37*   *58f. n.50, 76*
      5:17:2-4   *18*   Apostolic Constitutions
Council of Nicaea   Book 8, section 4   *61*
  Canon 4   *61*   Apostolic Canons
Canons of Hippolytus   Canon 1   *61*

FOURTH TO FIFTH CENTURY

Jerome   *10, 23, 24 n.13*   Chrysostom   *24 n.13*
  Epistle 146, To Evangelus   Theodore of Mopsuestia   *24 n.13*
      58 & n.50

FIFTH CENTURY

Council of Chalcedon
  Canon 6   *56 n.47*

4. INDEX OF NAMES AND SUBJECTS

Absolution   *6, 75f. n.60*   *am ha-aretz* see 'People of the land'
Alexandria, church of   *58 & n.50*   Ammia   *18*
Allen R.   *51*   Anti-clericalism see Clericalism

Apollos *53*
Apostolic Age *9f.*
archisunagogos see Synagogue-ruler
archons see Rulers
Attendant *(hazzan)* *34f. n.24, 35f.,
    37, 67f. & n.59*

Baptism *25, 51 n.43, 57 n.48,
    69f., 73, 74*
Baptists *38n.28*
Barlea O. *40*
Barnabas *20 n.10, 53*
Beckwith, R.T. *32 n.21*
beth ha-midrash *32*
Bingham J. *57 n.49*
Bishops *23f., 34f. n.24, 47-9 &
    n.40, 55-63 & n.50, 78*
Bradshaw P.F. *60 n.51*
Burtchaell J.T. *15, 34f. n.24*

Calvin J. *50f. n.42, 52 n.46*
Campbell R.A. *22 n.11*
Celibacy *79f.*
Chadwick H. *19 n.9, 58 n.50, 76
    n.61*
Chair, teaching *40f., 60f., 63*
Charismatic gifts *15-20, 47, 76f.*
Charismatic Movement *7, 16*
Charity, distribution of *43f., 66*
Charity treasurers *36, 43f.*
Clericalism, Anti-clericalism *6, 7,
    76f.*
Collins J.N. *16 n.6, 65*
Common Prayer, Book of *8, 9f.,
    11 n.1, 13, 81 n.63*
Communion, Holy *6, 13f., 25, 26,
    57f., 70-2, 75f., 81f., 83*
Congregationalists *38n.28*
Cranmer T. *8, 12f., 78 n.62*
Customs, primitive Christian *13f.*

Daube D. *40, 43 & n.35, 52 & n.46*
Deacons *11f., 20-2, 42f., 60 & n.53,
    64-8 & n.59, 79, 83*

Delorme J. *18 n.8*
Diotrephes *25*
Discipline, Christian *13, 57-9*
Dix G. *65 n.56*

Elders or Presbyters
    29 n.17, 81, 83f.
    See also Presbyter-Bishops
Elders, Jewish *22, 28-41 & nn.17,
    18;*
    training of *37-9;*
    as judges *33f., 39 n.29*
Elders, Christian *20-2, 44-8;*
    Jesus and his apostles as
        44f. & n.37, 84
Episcopal Ministry *13 n.3*
Eucharist see Communion, Holy
Ezra *30, 31 n.19*

Farrer A.M. *24*
Ferguson E. *40*
For Such a Time as This *83n.64*

Gamaliel I, Rabban *37, 46*
Gamaliel II, Rabban *37f.*

Hands, imposition of *37-41 & n.30,
    52-4, 61f., 83n.64*
Hanson R.P.C. *62 n.54*
Harnack A. von *17 n.7, 24 n.14*
Hatch E. *24 n.14*
hazzan see Attendant
Hoffman L.A. *40*
Hooker R. *8, 10, 13 n.3, 44 n.37,
    51 n.43, 78 n.62*

Institutional ministries *20-2,
    48 n.41*
Institutionalization *7*

Jalland T.G. *24 n.13, 26 n.16*
James the Lord's brother *20 n.10,
    23, 45, 55, 59*
Jerusalem 'council' *47, 50*

Jewel J.   *11 n.1*
John the apostle   *9, 23f., 25, 44 n.37*
John the Elder   *44 n.37*
Judges   *28-30, 33f., 38, 49f.*
  see also Lawyers

Kalsbach A.   *67 n.58*
Kilmartin E.J.   *40 n.34*
Kirk K.E.   *23 n.12, 24-7 & n.13,*
  26 n.16, 65 n.56

Laity, ministry of   *6f., 15f. & n.6,*
  26 n.16, 71, 72f., 76f., 81, 82f.
Lawyers   *22, 31*
Lay voice in ordinations   *58f. n.50,*
  78 & n.62
Levine L.I.   *31f. nn.18, 20, 22,*
  34f. n.24
Lightfoot J.B.   *23f. & nn.12, 13,*
  26f., 67
Lightfoot and Harmer   *45 n.38*

Martimort A.G.   *67 n.58*
Montanists   *19*

Newman J.   *38ff. nn.27, 29, 30*
Non-episcopal ministries   *82*
Non-Stipendiary Ministers   *51 n.44,*
  77

Ordination, rabbinical   *37-41, 56f.;*
  dispensability of   *39 & n.29, 82*
Ordination, Christian   *51, 52-4, 56f.,*
  58f., 64, 82;
  without title   *56f. & n.47;*
  indelibility of   *38 n.28;*
  non-episcopal   *78 n.62, 82*
Ordination, age at   *28-30, 80*
Ordination by three   *37, 61f., 78*
Ordination, female   *5f., 64 n.55, 67,*
  79, 83
Oversight, pastoral   *47-50, 59f., 81,*
  82f.

'People of the land' *(am ha-aretz)*
  36 & n.25
Pharisees   *32f. & n.21*
Philip the evangelist   *42, 53*
Pliny the Younger   *67*
Prayer   *34f., 55f., 66, 72f.*
Presbyterate, plural and sole   *55, 77*
Presbyters
  see Elders, Presbyter-Bishops
Presbyter-Bishops   *11-13, 20-2,*
  23-6 & nn.13, 14, 42-54, 72-4,
  82f.;
  qualifications for appointment
    50f.,65;
  training of   *45-7, cf.80;*
  duty of service   *51f.*
Presbyterians   *13, 50f. n.42*
Priests and Levites, as teachers
  30f., 83;
  as rulers and judges   *29, 33;*
  as ministers of ceremonies
    30, 73
Priesthood, ministerial   *11 n.1,*
  26 n.16, 60 & n.52, 74, 75, 83
Professionalization   *80*
Prophecy   *18f., 26 n.16*

Quadratus   *18*

'Rabbi' as title   *31, 39, 44*
Rabbinovitz L.I.   *31 n.18*
Reader   *76, 83n.64*
Reviv H.   *29 n.17*
Robinson D.W.B.   *16 n.6*
Robinson, J. Armitage   *16*
Rulers *(archons)*   *34f. & n.24, 36f.*
'Ruling elders'   *50f. n.42*
Ryle H.E.   *67*

Sacraments, ministry of   *24-6,*
  51 & n.43, 69-74, 75f.
Sanhedrin   *33f.*
Schams C.   *31 n.19*
Schweizer E.   *18 n.8*

Scribes   *22, 30-2 & n.19, 44*
Secularism   *7f.*
Seven, The   *42f., 45f. & n.39, 66*
Silas   *53*
Stott J.R.W.   *16*
Strack-Billerbeck   *61*
Subdeacons   *12, 66 n.57, 76*
Swete H.B.   *23 n.12, 62 n.54*
Synagogue   *30-6, 38, 43*
Synagogue-ruler *(archisunagogos)*
   34-6 & nn.24, 25, 55f.
Targums   *32, 35*
Teachers of the Law   *22, 31*
Teaching   *22, 30-3, 47f.,*
   59f. & n.51, 75f., 80, 81-3

Thirty-nine Articles   *8, 78 n.62*
Timothy and Titus   *25, 38 n.28,*
   52-4, 56
Tradition   *38, 44, 62 & n.54*
Trent, Council of   *6, 12, 75f. n.60*
Turner C.H.   *62 n.54*
Turner H.J.M.   *46 n.39*

Unity, preservation of   *13, 58 n.50*

Vermes G.   *47f. n.40*

Whitgift J.   *11 n.1*
Wise men, sages   *30, 31 nn.18, 19,*
   44